LAKE GARDA

BONECHI

© Copyright
CASA EDITRICE BONECHI
Via Cairoli 18/b
50131 Florence - Italy
e-mail: bonechi@bonechi.it
Internet: www.bonechi.com

Text and Editing: Giuliano Valdes,
Editing Studio-Pisa.

English translation by Rhiannon Lewis.

The photographs are the property of
the Archives of Casa Editrice Bonechi
and were taken by Studio Di Giovine Fotografica - Verona.
Photographer Western Bank: Luigi Di Giovine.
Photographer Eastern Bank: Giuseppe Bardaro.

We are grateful to 'Rivetta Souvenir snc' for
their generous assistance with the illustrations.

The publisher apologises for any omissions
and is willing to make amends with the formal recognition
of the author of any photo subsequently identified.

ISBN 978-88-7009-261-5

A 10 9 8 7 6 5 4 3 2 1

INTRODUCTION

The lake of Garda holds a post of absolute supremacy amongst the articulated and diverse tourist attractions in the sub alpine regions. Situated between three areas which are geographically well-defined: Lombardia, Veneto and Trentino-Alto Adige, the largest of the Italian lake basins it is essentially a Mediterranean dream. The vast mirrors of its turquoise and transparent waters, perennially wrinkled by winds which sometimes blow with such intensity that real tempests are stirred up, giving the lake an image of a "sea" as the great poet of the Latinity Publio Virgilio Marone defined it two thousand years ago. In fact there are few territories in Italy which present such a vast diversity of landscapes as that of Garda: the scenic perspectives change at every corner mingling in a phantasmagorical harmony of chromatic tonality, of lights, of sounds, of perfumes and of confined and disquieting silences. If Garda is sometimes referred only by its antomasia of "lake" it shows that it has made a permament impression in the spirit and in the human soul, attracting many illustrious literary men, poets and men of letters who have all rendered it immortal from the dawining of civilization. Amongst the numerous personalities who have been struck by the beauty of this monument to nature, emerges the figure of J. Wolfgang Goethe, the author of "Journey in Italy", who, in 1786, travelling around the shores of the lake, marked the beginning of modern tourism. We have said at the beginning that Garda is a Mediterranaen dream; this can be repeated with the conviction that as such it must appear to travellers and tourists who come from the northern countries. Let us for just one moment try to immagine the sensations, the emotions, the astonishment, the ecstacy of someone who finds himself contemplating the Garda landscape for the very first time, still having impressed in his mind the cold and flat monotonous tonality of a landscape characterized by the perennial mists and depressing greyness of earth and sky. Crossing the bends of the Nago, in the direction of Torbole an oasis of intense azzurre opens out, as if by magic in which are reflected the green impending profile of the Rocchetta, the mountains of Riva and other reliefs which face onto the western part of Garda. Lower down, on the right, can be seen the houses of Torbole and a thin strip of flat lake, between the characteristic profile of Mount Brione and the geologically interesting reliefs, which rise up behind Torbole. Proceeding in a southerly direction the lake-side landscape maintains its substantially uniform characteristics, despite the multiplicity of various views which present themselves to whoever goes along the coastal road for the first time. At this point the Garda basin takes on the form of a narrow funnel which seems to be wedged in between the pre-alpine formations. With an imaginary line which joins the two areas of Garda, between Maderno and Torri del Benaco, the horizon of the lake, gradually but constantly widens out until it finally takes on marine dimensions in the southern part, surrounded by the gentle and fertile morainic slopes of the Po valley near Brescia, of the Valténesi and of the moranic amphitheatre in the Verona region. Over everything dominates the great majesty of the "king" Garda, which towers over the upper margin of the plain, under the watchful gaze of Mount Baldo which rises on the right, almost like a natural and faithful sentry, covered up until the springtime by a spotless cloak of snow. In this land of fairy tales and dreams, recurrs the Mediterranean element which thrives, almost like a magical spell, in the luxuriant olive groves and in the thriving lemon groves, in the rows of vines, in the green and scenic sequences of cypress trees, in the mild air, in the perfume of the flowers, in the ski-blue luminosity of the sky. This Mediterranean margin, uniquely reproduced between the plains of the Po valley and of the Dolomites, is one of the most sought after spots by tourists and holiday-makers from beyond the Alps and represents one of the most characteristic signs of the Insubri regions, loved and visited even by Italian tourist, chiefly because of its notable importance in the boundless touristic patrimony of our country. From an administrative point of view the Lake of Garda is divided amongst the provinces of Brescia (Lombardy), Trento (Trentino-Alto Adige) and Verona (Veneto). Its average height is 65 metres above sea level; its surface area is 370 sq.kilometres, while the maximum depth reaches 346 metres. The perimetre of the lake is 155 kilometres, its length varies between 3 and 17.5 Kms while its length between Riva and Peschiera reaches 51.6 kms. The transparency of its crystalline waters allows a visibility of around 15 metres. The pleasant coastal climate allows for enjoyable stays in each season of the year and permits the flourishing of Mediterranean trees and flowers. The marine fauna includes eels, trouts, pikes and other fresh water fish while the avifauna includes wild ducks, herons and moorhens. Due to its central position between the plains of the Po basin and the Pre-Alps, it is easily reached by means of any of the comunication systems. The geological formation of Garda goes back to the post-Mioecene era and to the complicated vicissitudes of the glaciation which took place in the region of the river Adige and that of Brenta. Traces of this can be seen in the morphology of the mountain rocks which surround the upper portion of the lake and on the Morenic hills which border the southern margin. Its principal tributary/emissary is the Sarca-Mincio. Its most important islands are those of Garda, San Biagio, Trimelone, Sogno and Olivo.
Amongst the recurring winds we should note the Sòver (Tramontana), the Ora (Ostro), the Vinezza (Scirocco) and the Ander (Libeccio).
Already established in pre-historic times, the Garda territory was then populated by Venetians, Ligurians, Etruscans and Gauls. In Roman times it was known as Benacus lacus - from which it gets its modern name of Benaco - then it was conquered by the Longobards. The place name of Garda appeared in the Carlovingian era, when the town of the same name was raised to the rank of county. Bitterly fought over by the Venetians and the Viscontis (15th century) it was for a long time under the control of the former. After the Napoleonic parenthesis the Congress of Vienna ratified the dependence of the region of Austria.

SIRMIONE

The Gem of the Peninsula, according to a definition by Caio Valerio Catullo, illustrious poet of the latinity, stretches out along the lower basin of Garda, along the southern margin of the Brescia territory. The thin little peninsula reaches a length of 4 kilometres and in the thinnest parts measures only 120 metres; with its unmistakeable profile it constitutes one of the most characteristic landscapes between Desenzano and Peschiera where it forms the division between the two gulfs. The town was already famous in Roman times as *Sermio Mansio* and it soon became a favourite spot with the wealthier members of the Roman society, attracted by the beauty of the place and the extraordinary mild lake-side climate. Even today the numerous traces left over from the Roman age make it an important stop on tourist itineraries. Due to the characteristics of its position it played an essentially important role, both in terms of defence and strategy, even under the Byzantines and the Longobards. Established as a free Commune, it soon became subjected to the Scaligeri of Verona who saw to the fortification of the town and the building of a turretted battlemented fortress which today has become the most noted tourist spot in Sirmione. In the first years of the 15th century the small fortified nucleus became a part of the territories governed by the extremely

powerful Republic of San Marco. Sirmione nowadays is a lively tourist town in the southern part of Garda, and has become a popular health resort and summer holiday place. The centre of the town used to be the location of ancient thermal baths, which date back to remote times - it seems that the so - called *Grottoes of Catullo* are none other than the ruins of thermal bath buildings of the Roman period - and take advantage of the waters which flow from the *Thermal font of Boiola*. This is in fact an underwater spring which originates from the lake a few hundred metres east of the peninsula. The thermal waters then flow into the thermal buildings in the centre and are used to cure deafness. The waters can cure illnesses such as rheumatism, arthritis, respiratorial problems and also for disturbances in the female genital system, and also skin disorders. Sirmione has managed to conserve an urban dimension which keeps pace with modern man, made easy by the labyrinth of streets and characteristic alleys which are strictly pedestrian and crowded by a composite number of tourists and visitors. The little centre has been able to harmonize and keep in equilibrium the stamp of an urban town of ancient origins with the more recent areas of building expansion. All of this is brought to life by the blazing and flashing characteristics of the picturesque dock, in which the battlemented castle is reflected and by the lush vegetation which represents one of the most notable aspects of the town.

Left, a view of the peninsula of Sirmione; above, the town with the Scaligera Fortress and the harbour.

Above: Sirmione, the Scaligera Fortress and the entrance bridge; the merlons and the towers of the Fortress (adjacent).

THE SCALIGERA FORTRESS

The Rocca Scaligera is the most interesting tourist attraction in Sirmione. It was built in the second half of the 13th century, commisioned by Mastino Della Scala the First, a lord of Verona. It is surrounded by the waters of the lake which unite with the internal dock. The towers set at each corner, the double line of tower walls, crowned by Ghibelline merlons and the outstanding central keep which culminates in brackets which sustain the sequence of merlons, giving the whole complex the appearance of an imposing fortified structure, rich in historical associations. Within the walled enclosure which is accessible only by two drawbridges, we find the *lapidario romano e medievale* (the Roman and Medieval lapidary), which is of considerable archeological interest. The sentry walks around the walls, the towers and the

Above: Sirmione, the small evocative square which leads to the Fortress; the drawbridge (adjacent).

On the following pages: Sirmione, other views of the imposing Scaligera fortification, detail of the internal river basin facing the lake and a view of the peninsula from the main tower of the Fortress.

raised central keep are splendid scenic lookout posts from where the view stretches over the town, its peninsula, and the magnificent lake.

Entry into the historical nucleus of Sirmione is made through a gate which forms part of the Scaligero complex and which leads into the intricate but evocative labyrinth of narrow medieval lanes. These are brightened up by interesting architectural elements, while on the ground floor of the building we can find artesan workshops, typical houses and many souvenir stands and restaurants where it is possible to taste the specialities of the typical Garda cuisine. Elegant buildings and well-preserved houses face the few piazza and open spaces of the town; rows of small tables sheltered by colourful umbrellas are meeting points or places where the visitor can interupt his tourist itinerary, taking advantage of the bars and refreshment stands.

Above: Sirmione, the river basin and the Scaligera Fortress by night; examples of Medieval architecture in the lanes of the historic town centre (adjacent).

THE CHURCH OF ST. PETER IN MAVINO

In the upper part of the town stands the Church of St. Peter in Mavino. This beautiful place of worship is set in a pleasant scenic spot, at the edge of a thick olive grove, with evocative parnoramic views. The first construction was completed in early medieval times where once stood a site of pagan worship. In the 11th century the church was completedly reconstructed with a bell-tower; new work was carried out in the course of the 14th century. The church, as it stands today, is a simple linear

Above: Sirmione, one of the colourful squares in the town centre; the Bell dedicated to the Fallen and the façade of the Church of St. Peter in Mavino (adjacent).

building; on the piazza which the church looks out onto can be found, amonst the olive trees, the modern votive altar with the *Bell dedicated to the Fallen*. The external apse dominated by a small bell-tower, is elegant and interesting: the central apse is framed by two smaller apses. The interior which is extremely cosy is made up of one nave and was decorated with frescoes during the 13th to 16th centuries. Particularly worthy of mention are the frescoes which adorn the vault and the walls of the main apse, above which a beautiful wooden *Crucifix* can be seen.

Adjacent: Sirmione, the Church of St. Peter in Mavino, detail of the main apse and frescoes and a view of the interior (below).

THE CHURCH OF SANTA MARIA MAGGIORE

The Church of Santa Maria Maggiore is situated near the Rocca Scaligera and is preceded by a porch held up by columns. The first column on the left is in fact a Roman milestone dating back to the 4th century A, D, and is known as the *milestone of Giuliano the Apostate*. The building, of the 15th century, stands on the site of a pagan temple: the interior, which has only one nave, is in the Late Gothic style. Among the various works of art stand out, in the apse, the wooden pulpit and choir stalls, which are the result of work carried out by able 17th century engravers. We should also mention the 15th century wooden statue of the *Madonna*, the 15th - 16th century frescoes and a valuable painting in the Venetian style depicting the *Apostles' Supper*.

Sirmione: the Church of St. Mary the Greater, a view of the façade and of the portico (adjacent); detail of the Milestone of Giuliano the Apostate (below left) and detail of the frescoes in the interior.

THE CHURCH OF ST. ANNA

The small Church of St. Anna, which is also close to the fortress, is a 17th century building and it catches the visitor's eye because of its refined ornate baroque plan. The vault over the altar is particularly interesting, and here we can see where the effect of architectural lines is harmoniously united with the stucco work - of exquisite workmanship, with the painting and with the sculptures. In the church traces of valuable 16th century frescoes are still visible.

Adjacent: Sirmione, the façade of the Church of St. Anne; detail of the interior vaults and of the main altar (below).

Above, an aerial view of the Grottoes of Catullo; right, part of the delightful olive grove that leads to the archaeological site.

THE GROTTOES OF CATULLO

The archeological complex of the so-called *grottoes* of Catullo occupy the northernmost part of the evocative peninsula stretching scenically out into the turquoise waters of the lower Garda basin. All this area is submerged in a landscape of extreme evocativeness; particularly at sunset the effect of light and burning tonality that penetrates the ancient ruins, immersed in the dominant greenness of the olive groves which have as a natural background rows of proud cypress trees, standing like sentries in the impending obsurity of the night, gives an effect with is exceedingly picturesque and dramatic. Towards the slopes that descend gradually towards the lake one often comes across the outline a little sad, but also very decorative, of the willow trees which make up an extremely typical and recurring characteristic of the southernmost

*The Grottoes of Catullo with part of the lake;
some of the impressive Roman remains (facing page).*

coast of Garda (Benaco). The Grottoes of Catullo are among the largest and most representative archeological sights discovered in northern Italy and in particular the Insubri (Lombardy) region. The name of *Grotto* is most unsuitable as the large surface restored for the enjoyment of tourists and archeologists refers, in all probability, to a magnificent Roman residential complex of the Imperial age which also incorporated conspicuous remains of a thermal bath building and some shop premises which would suggest the reason for the incorrect name. The date on the building is both uncertain and contradictory: archeological digs carried out on the part which is considered to be the oldest (the southern part) would suggest a building which could be placed as being built in the 1st century B.C. The archeological zone consists of a large rectangle (167.44 × 105.56 m) faced by a forepart towards the ground of 43 × 32.26 m. Altogether the complex of this huge villa occupies a surface area of 20345 sq.m and stretches, from north to south up to 240.90 m. It appears certain that the building was carried out in two separate eras; remarkable archeological findings led by Prof. M. Mirabella Roberti, during excavation work carried out in the 1950's are arranged in an *Antiquarium* which one can visit, which is near the entrance. On show are framgents of sculptures, pieces of mosaics, remains of frescoes, oil lamps, jewels and other findings. The numerous places in the archeological complex offer the occasion for a historical and literary visit to this strip of territory near Brescia, permeated by the quotations of Catullo who lived here for a long time, writing verses which praise the beauty of the lake. The *Big Olive Grove, The Street of the Shops, The Big Pillar, The Three-Mullioned Window of Paradise, The Grotta of Cavallo* (a vaulted subterranean cavity), *The Room of the Giants, The Double Criptoporticus, The Bathroom, The Swimming pool* and the *Cister* believed to make up part of the thermal bath building - all constitute an obligatory itinerary engulfed in historical reminiscences and literary and scenic suggestions.

SAN MARTINO DELLA BATTAGLIA

The town is set on hilly spurs of Morainic origin which define the limits, like an amphitheatre, of the strip of land to the south of the lake. In this territory on the 24th June 1859 the Piedmontese inflicted a decisive defeat on the Austrians which marked the destiny of the Second War of Independence. The battle brought about an enormus sacrifice of human life which is recorded for ever in the mighty **Panoramic Tower** which rises up on top of a hill, and with a height of 64,60 m dominates the land around it. The building was erected between 1890 and 1893, based on a project by the Bergamasque architect Frizzoni. Over the Tower there is a lighthouse which during the night radiates tri-coloured lights inside which can be seen frescoes depicting episodes from the Risorgimento, objects, historical momentoes, relics and souvenirs of the battle. In the vicinity of the tower one can visit the **History Museum** finished at the end of the 1930's. In the *Chapel of the Treccani Counts* we can see the **Ossario** (ossuary) which holds the mortal remains of a great number of fallen soldiers.

POZZOLENGO

This charming place in the Morainic amphitheatre of Garda has origins which probably go back to Celtic times (5th century B.C.) and was an important refeshment place in Roman times when *Pocelingus* was skirted by a major road. Here Attila camped before moving against

Rome (5th century). The **Abbey of San Vigilio** (12th century) was built by the Vallombrosan and is still in an excellent state of conservation.

Of an early medieval **Castle** only a few traces of the restructuring carried out between the 13th, 14th and 15th centuries remain. The **Church of San Lorenzo Martire** (18th century) which shows artistic elements of great worth and paintings by Andrea Celesti and Brusasorci, and the 16th century **Gelmetti Palace** are also very interesting.

SOLFERINO

The town in the Province of Mantua stands on the external limit of the Morainic amphitheatre of Garda and dominates the land in the Piedmont part of the Po valley. Its historical importance is due to the epic battle which was carried out here on 24th June 1859 at the same time as that of San Martino, between the French troops and the Austrian army during the Second War of Independence. The French were led by Napoleon Third and the Austrians by "Kaiser" Francesco Giuseppe who had marshalled his troops into two corps assuming the direction of the military operations. The battle was bitterly fought along a strip of land which is included between where the Chiese and the Mincio rivers run, in an area where the neighbouring town of Peschiera played the role of one of the vertices and one of the most significant

Above: San Martino della Battaglia, the memorial tower; a panoramic view of Pozzolengo.

strong holds in the powerful and almost impregnable Austrian defensive apparatus and which has come down through history known as "Quadrilatero". The battle was divided into two sections: in the morning the proceedings were substantially uncertain and well-balanced; but the conclusion came in the first hours of the afternoon with the conquest of important positions carried out by the French. Towards 4 o'clock in the afternoon the Emperor Francesco Giuseppe ordered the withdrawal of his troops having understood the impossibility of reversing the situation, which in fact was extremely unfavourable. During the battle the French had 80,000 soldiers with 240 pieces of artillery while the Austrians, quantitively and qualitively superior, went into battle with 90,000 men and 309 pieces of artillery. At the end 33,000 men were killed or wounded on both the opposing sides.

From the *Castle Square*, passing under an ancient arch, we come to the huge **Tower** which is surmounted by a beautiful dome opened at the lower part by small arches supported by elegant pillars. A plaque bears the following words: "This Tower built in the year 1563 by Orazio

Adjacent: Solferino, the memorial tower; the Italian Red Cross Memorial (below).

Gonzaga, the first lord of the area to defend the dwelling and its prestige. After various vicissitudes of time, of men and of things, the Solfinerese had it restored, to hand it over in a safe condition to future generations who can build their present, knowing and meditating on the pages of their past. Year 1979''.

The **Memorial to the Italian Red Cross** is in honour of the institution set up by the Nobel Prize winner for peace (1901) J. Henri Dunant. The philanthropist from Geneva who witnessed great suffering on the part of the wounded in the battle of Solferino set up the organization of the *Red Cross* which has since become one of the most humanitarian institutions which helps man during natural disasters and during war time events. The **Ossuary** is contained within the chapel of the *Church of St. Peter* which has an elegant front in three orders decorated by statues and decorative motifs and vertically incised by pilastre strips. The **History of the Battle Museum** is to be found in the low building which has arches in front of it. Here one can find pieces of artillery, banners, paintings, prints, relics and various objects dating back to the famous battle.

Adjacent: Solferino, the façade and the interior of the Ossuary (below); on the opposite page, one of the rooms of the Battle Museum and a view of the entrance.

DESENZANO DEL GARDA

This beautiful small town is considered to be one of the pearls of the Brescian coast of Garda and it charmingly faces the lake, at the foot of the Morainic hills that descend onto the western gulf of Garda, formed by the peninsula of Sirmione and by the Punta del Vo.

The first origins of Desenzano seem to date back to a pile-dweller seat established during the Bronze Age (the 21st to 29th century B.C.). Archeological findings support the hypothesis that the primitive cultural manifestations belong to the civilisations of Polada (near Brescia), largely spread out over the Po valley, the Veneto and the Piedmont area. The place name of Desenzano is of evident Roman origin and refers to the *fundus Decentianus*: for certain it is well known that in Roman times it was one of the favourite towns of the Capitolini family who have left their traces in a huge villa and a large number of archeological vestices. In medieval times Desenzano was an attractive centre for the inhabitants of the nearby cities of Verona and Brescia who fought for a long time over its control. Beginning from the first half of the 15th century the town became part of the territories administrated by the Republic of San Marco enjoying a prosperous and flourishing economic development, which was also determined by the important role carried out by the local wheat market whose quotations set up a strong parametre through a vast area. The Desenzano of today is an appreciated and frequented tourist spot, rich in elements of substantial urban interest, of archtectural interest, and of historic and artistic interest. The pleasant coastal climate accounts for the luxuriant development of a lush vegetation which includes typical species of the Mediterranean latitudes, as for example the laurel, the olive, the palm tree and the oleander. The neighbouring territory consists of extensive hilly areas which form the ideal habitat for wine growing; especially famous are the Lugana and the Tocai. For the same climatic reasons Desenzano is a famous holiday locality, a spot where tourists come throughout each season of the year, endowed with a practical tourist dock it is a major port for lake navigation services and has developed activities in the service sector and also has excellent connections with the motorway network of the Po valley.

In the centre of the town we come to the *Malvezzi Square* which is rich in extremely interesting enviromental motifs. The **former town hall building** looks out onto the ancient dock which penetrates into the town and was built by Giulio Todeschini. In the background of the piazza which is dominated by *the monument to Angela Merici* (from the 15th to the 16th centuries) born here and

Above and following page, top, two views of the harbour; below right, the monument to Angela Merici; left, the little lighthouse.

22

founder of the Ursuline Order, the turretted mass of the Medieval **Castle** rises up on the site of a Roman *Castrum* of which remain only the imposing walls and towers. The **Church of Santa Maria Maddalena** dates back to the 16th century and was built by the architect Giulio Todeschini. The interior divided into three naves holds an important, painting called *The Last Supper* painted by Tiepolo, paintings by Zenon Veronese, by Celesti and by other masters. In the **Bagatta Palace**, which has now become the town hall, one can admire the *Deposition* of excellent artistic value, believed to be the work of Palma the Younger. The Roman origins of Desenzano can be seen, in an unparalleled way, when one visits the **Villa Romana** (the Roman Villa) of the 3rd to 5th centuries, discovered at the beginning of the 1920's. The ruins, which are of particular architectural interest, permit us to reconstruct in our minds the various rooms from *the octagon, the peristyle, the room of apses, the ninpheus, the library*, to *the tablinum*. The most outstanding element are the marvellous **mosaic floors** depicting allegorical scenes, geometric motifs and hunting and fishing scenes that catch the eye for their lively chromatic tonality.

ANTIQUARIUM

Since 1971 an antiquarium has been situated in a building in the immediate vicinity of the Roman Villa where we can find numerous archeological remains found in the *Borgo Regio* which makes up one of the oldest areas of the town, most probably of Roman origin. Amongst the numerous findings in the show cases there are pieces of sculpture, oil lamps, amphorae, bronze utensils, architectural elements, the remains of a pluteno and small millstones. Amongst the most representative objects is a *Bacco bambino* (Bacchus as a child) carried out between the 1st and 2nd centuries A.C., a Bacchus copied from a Hellenistic original, *a bust of a boy with a crown* (4th century A.D.), an a glass ball and decorative *pieces of mosaic flooring*.
Along the lakeside gardens can be seen the so-called **Sarcophagus of Atilia Urbica** urns made of white stone with "roof like" covers in red Veronese marble, decorated with reliefs and epigraphs. The last traces of the Roman presence at Desenzano can be found in the *building with apses* of the second half of the 4th century and by a building in which were discovered in 1970, five *mosaic floorstones* one on top of the other, which can be dated back to between the 1st century B.C. and the 1st century A.D.

PADENGHE SUL GARDA

A pleasant hilly spot, crowned by an ancient castle, this town is situated at the southernmost limit of the Valtenesi in an open position on the south western gulf of Garda (Benaco), defined at the horizon by the thin peninsula of Sirmione. From the hill, on a clear day, one can see far into the distance, well beyond the relatively near Desenzano as far as Sirmione, Peschiera, Garda and other towns in the Garda region of Verona. The origins of the place date back to the Roman period when it became a favourite spot of the noble families close to the Milanese imperial who built magnificient dwellings and places of worship. The Roman *Patingulae*, built between the 3rd

Adjacent: Desenzano, characteristic views of the historic town centre; below, the Antiquarium, Bacchus the Child; on the opposite page, detail of the decorated mosaic floors.

and the 4th centuries became famous for its functioning port, considered as being one of the most important in the entire lakeside basin. Around the 11th century stood a castle which later became a defensive bulwark which was of extreme importance for the lakeside seats seriously threatened by the Barbaric invaders. In medieval times Patingulae was subjected to feudal quarrels between the Guelfa and Ghibellina families. Afterwards it passed under the control of the Serene Republic of San Marco, it ended up following the historical vicissitudes of the Brescian region of Garda. Padenghe is the native town of the 16th to 17th century painter Giovanni Andrea Bertanza, who has left numerous traces of his work in the whole Garda area, in particular at Salò.

The Padenghe of today can be seen as a charming residential unity made up of villas and dwellings which gradually go down as far as the lake, which once again heightens the charm of the lake which had been abandoned in the early Middle Ages when the hills were believed to be more secure because of the castle that protected them. Around the lake we can now see a modern beach which is well-equipped for bathing facilities and is provided with modern harbour equipment for touristst (*West Garda*). In the area we can also find a tourist centre which has a considerably important role for summer holidays and for the so-called "congress" tourists. The ancient centre is set out on the slope of a hill, pleasantly marked by rows of vines, by olive groves and by the noble outline of the dark green cypress trees. On the whole, the economy of the town, obtained purely by tourist and residential activities, de-

Adjacent: Padenghe sul Garda, panorma of the town dominated by the Castle; a view of the interior of the walls and the apse of the Church of St. Emiliano (below).

notes typical rural activities linked to the cultivation of olive trees and vines which in this area of the Valtenesi produces wines of remarkable quality such as the Trebbiano di Padenghe, the Tocai and the Pinot.

The **Castle** was originally erected in the 11th century and was then reconstructed in the period when Communal autonomy was flourishing. In the ancient ruins one can see the enclosure walls, partly battlemented, the corner towers and a quadrilateral tower/dungeon. One can visit the internal nucleus of the Castle, where the ancient houses are still to be seen. The small **Church of S. Emiliano** is placed in an evocative landscape, dominated by the lively chromatic shades of the lake which here form a contrast with the greenery of the surrounding hills. This small church, of a single aisle, which dates back to the 12th century, is a beautiful example of Romanesque Art, built completely of huge square blocks of stone. Particularly evocative is the portion of the apse, decorated on the higher part by a sequence of small arches and dominated by a small bell-tower in the shape of a bell.

The **Church of Saint Mary** is a pleasant construction which has a bright front consisting of two orders surmounting a triangular tympanum, decorated with niches full of statues and marked on the lower part by pilaster strips. A few decorations on the façade show its Baroque origins which date back to the second half of the 17th century. The interior has some interesting paintings and sculptures amongst which we should note the altarpiece attributed to Andrea Celesti, the *Saint Anthony the Abbot* by Francesco Paglia; *the Madonna of the Seven Sufferings and four Saints* by Francesco Zugno; the *Saint Christopher and the Virgin with Saints Rocco, Sebastian and Anthony the Abbot* by Zenon Veronese; the altarpiece depicting *Saints Rocco, Sebastian and Donors*, believed to be the work of Torbido; the *Virgin in Glory with Saint Emiliano and other Saints* by Paolo Farinati; the two sculptures depicting *Humility* and *Temperance*, by the artist from Brescia Antonio Calegari.

In the vicinity of the town rises, in the greenery of an olive grove, the imposing battlemented outline of the **Drugolo Castle**. The construction which is extremely ancient, has been considerably changed throughout the ages by numerous reconstructions, the last of which dates back to the 1930's. The building, built in huge blocks of stone, is a quadrilateral mass, crowned by Ghibelline merlons and reinforced by corner towers and brackets.

MONIGA DEL GARDA

The town was an important medieval settlement, still partially included in its own castle walls, which picturesquely face the hilly spurs of the Valtenesi, in an excellent panoramic position which looks out onto the outstretched mirror of the Garda lakeside. The outstandingly typical characteristics of the Garda landscape that acquire a particularly sweet and charming note in this southern part of the lake, form an admirable "crown" for this spot. Being a rich tapestry of wine cultivation - Moniga is an area where famous wines are produced, for example the Rosato, the Rosso di Moniga and the Chiaretto - dotted here and there by the olive groves, whilst the cypress trees, the laurel trees and the oleander further enliven the strong colours of the landscape which offer outstanding scenic

Padenghe sul Garda: the Drugolo Castle and the Parish Church of St. Mary.

On the opposite page: two views of the picturesque gulf of Padenghe looking out towards the peninsula of Sirmione (below); the Castle of Moniga del Garda (above) and a detail of the Castle of Padenghe (adjacent).

views. The first establishments in this portion of the Garda territory go back to the First Bronze Age (21st to the 29th century B.C.) as has been ascertained by the discoveries on an outstretched pile-dweller seat on the margin of the lake, close to the port. The etymology of the place could be explained by an ancient sanctuary consecreated to the worship of the godess Diana Munichia. Without doubt the town was an important centre in Roman times given its vicinity to the Via Gallica, an important connection netween the territories of Brescia and those of Verona. Amongst the numerous Roman findings, which confirm the hypothesis of a settlement at this period, should be noted a pagan altar dating from the 4th to the 5th centuries discovered in the structure of the walls of an antique building in the early 1980's bearing an important epigraph. In the early Medieval Age Moniga was under the control of a Veronese monastic institution. Beginning from the 12th century the town became a feudal unity and therefore, became part of the lands dominated by Venice, up until the time of the fall of that glorious Republic. Today Moniga del Garda has become a part of the tourist circuit of Garda and is equipped with modern and functional hotel services. Hotels, camp-sites and restaurants typical of the area are able to receive numerous tourists, offering hospitality and the delicious characteric cuisine of the Garda area, which is based on fresh-water fish, rich in trout, eels and other lake fish. There is a dock which can

Moniga del Garda: the façade and the arcades of the Villa Bertanzi and its gardens (adjacent).

be used for tourist purposes on the lake, whilst the small port is a centre for lake-line connections.

The **Medieval Castle** is considered as being one of the most important buildings of the Valténesi, as far as architectural defence buildings are concerned. It has reached us in an excellent state of preservation and follows the forms of the *Castrum* of the Roman period with walls with fortifications crowned by merlons and reinforced by massive cylindrical towers. The Castle building has a rectangular plan; at the entrance, over which there is an arch, there rises the powerfull square tower of the 15th century that also has the function of a bell-tower. The buildings inside the castle walls are of extreme urban interest: some rows of houses, which lean against the enclosure walls and were originally secure shelters during the Dark Middle Ages. Outside the building, on the road that leads to the lake, is the beautiful 14th century **Church of Santa Maria della Neve**. The simple hut-like front is preceded by a pronaos of the 16th century and has a bas-relif which dates back to the 10th century. In an extremely scenic spot stands the little **Church of San Sivino** with its pronouced Romanesque characteristics. In the vicinity of the castle is the **Church of San Martino** (15th century), which has an architecturally elegant façade. The **Villa Bertanzi** (once known as *Brunati*) is an imposing 17th century building, characterised by the porch at the front of the building and by a beautiful park. Inside there are remarkable paintings of the modern Venetian school, which were collected by the historian P.G. Molmenti who lived here for a long time.

THE VALTÉNESI

From a geographic point of view Valténesi occupies a portion of the Brescian riviera of Garda which has Portese to the north of it and Padenghe sul Garda to the south of it. Padenghe sul Garda, Moniga, sul Garda, Soiano del Lago, Polpenazze del Garda, Puegnago, Manerba del Garda, S. Felice del Benaco, Portese, all constitute part of this area of the district. From a morphological and structural point of view the territory of Valténesi owes its varying shape to the complex geological events connected with the great glaciation and have taken the form of undulating hilly formations, originating from the deposits of the extensive Moraini glacic formations. These sediments have determined the formation

Valténesi: a view towards Soiano del Lago.

of a particularly fertile land, which has always been put to agricultural and viticultural use. It must be kept in mind that the Valténesi is one of the chief wine-growing areas of the province of Brescia: this is the area in which the Chiaretto is produced, one of the most important wines, but there are also other wines which should be mentioned such as Trebbiano di Padenghe, the Groppello Gentile, the Pinot, the Tocai, the Italian Riesling, the Rosato and the Rosso di Moniga, the Trebbiano di Polpenazze, the Berzamino, the Tocai Friulano di Puegnago, the Groppello and the Rosso di Manerba, the Tocai of San Felice del Benaco and other excellent wines. What characterises the landscape and environment of the Valténesi is the luxuriant and purely mediterranean vegetation: the olive groves which are alternated with rows of vines, give an oil of excellent quality. Proud and arrogant rows of cypresses arise here and there together with other sub-Alpine and mediterranean specimens and revive the delicate colours of ths countryside. The Valténesi.is also of great interest for archeologists who have found, during their excavations, conspicuous traces of not only the Roman period but also of other civilisations which date even further back.

Above: a panoramic view of Polpenazze del Garda; the façade of the Church of St. Mary (adjacent).

POLPENAZZE DEL GARDA

The town of Polpenazze is situated on the hills of the innermost part of the Valténesi with extensive panoramic views.

The historical centre is of evident medieval typology and is partially enclosed by the ancient castle walls which were nearly all destroyed during the 16th century. The only remaining element being a massive turretted structure which is conglobated in the town hall. The historical vicissitudes of the place seem to date back to Roman times, judging from the abundance of archeological findings in the territory. In the communal territory there can be found what remains of the ancient *Lucone lake* which was subjected to drainage during the second half of the 15th century. Along its banks traces of remote lake dwellings have been found. These dwellings are a common denominator of many of those in Lombardy. Substantial excavations conducted by the Gavardo Cave Group during the second half of the 1960's, have brought to light many archeological findings that date back to the Bronze Age (21st century B.C.). Amongst the most important findings there is a pirogue (now on show in the Museum of Gavardo), utensils, bowls and ceramics. In the locality of Bottenago have been found an epigraph and a Roman milestone and there is reason to believe that Bottenago was one of the most important human seats of the entire area of Valténesi. In this hamlet subjected to the Alens, as can be detected from the plaque which dates back to the 16th century existed up until the last century the Church of Santa Maria and a castle.

The **Church of Santa Maria** is a pleasantly situated building set in a scenic piazza and can be defined as a balcony overlooking the Garda and the Valténesi. The building which was finished at the end of the 16th century has a 10th century façade and a pronaos both of which recall Baroque motifs.

In the interior of the church can be seen numerous paintings of value including *The Madonna with Child* and *Two Warrior Saints* by Pietro Morone; the *Crucifixion* by Luigi Sigurtà; the *Birth of the Virgin* by Grazio Cossali; the *Assunta* attributed to Lucchese (Pietro Ricchi).

A little outside the town stands the Romanesque **Church of Saint Peter in Lucone** which stands out for its hut-like façade and has a rose window. The interior, divided into three parts, has gothic elements present in its architecture and has a high presbitary. Two frescoes, recently discovered depict *Christ among the Angels* (14th century) and *Saint Rocco* (15th century).

Polpenazze is the place of origin of the Bertolotti family, one of whose members was Gasparo da Salò, the inventor of the violin. In the surroundings, of extreme scenic interest, and for this reason a spot frequented by tourists, many flourishing tourist activities prosper mainly dedicated to the production of excellent wines of the area.

Adjacent: Polpenazze del Garda, the interior of the Church of St. Peter in Lucone; detail of the frescoes (below).

Above: hand-made vessels; a tomb with funeral ornaments (adjacent) in the Civic Palaentology Museum of Gavardo.

GAVARDO

Gavardo is an interesting little town situated at the mouth of the Val Sabbia, one of the three "valleys" of the Brescia area (by antonomasia), which look out onto the river Chiese. The town has several buildings of architectual value, which has some outstanding churches and historical buildings. In the district numerous archeological excavations have been carried out and have brought to light traces that date back to the Neolithic period, evidence of the Bronze Age, and material dating back to the Roman times and to the Barbaric period. During the Medieval Age, Gavardo endured various vicissitudes; at first controlled by the Brescians, it then became the possession of the della Scala family of Verona, of the Visconti family of Milan and the Republic of San Marco. At the time of the Risorgimento War the town was deprived of a beautiful medieval bridge, which in fact was blown up by the Austrians who intended to block off its access to the soldiers of Garibaldi. The element of greatest turist interest is without doubt the **Civic Museum of Palaeontology** which was founded in the second half of the 1950's by members of the local Cave Group. The museographic connection can be found in the *Castel of Dalla Via* which is built on a medieval plan. Amongst the various evidence that can be found there, the Prehistoric findings which come from the drained lake of Lucone near Polpenazze catch the eye. We can also find epigraphical material discovered on the site and in the nearby towns of Salò and of Lonato, collections of fossils and material brought to light near the so-called "Friar's Hole" where the skeletons of a wolf and a bear were found.

Above: the enchanting gulf of Manerba del Garda; the Fortress as seen from Porto S. Felice (adjacent).

MANERBA DEL GARDA

The hamlets that make up the commune of Manerba are set out along the central part of the Valténesi, that culminates on the characteristic promontary which delimits the western part of the wide gulf of Desenzano. This part of the charming valley of the Brescian coast was called in the past "Ateniese Valley", for the spectacular beauty of the nature and for the serene Mediterranean enviroment that recalls some characteristics of the Attic landscape. The name of the place seems to derive from *Minerva arx*, with obvious reference to the mighty fortress that once dominated the promontory. In the district traces of Gallic and Roman settlements have been found and have provided interesting archeological records. It seems quite certain that this was a favourite place with the Roman nobles who, for their stays here, constructed sumptious residences. The promontory of Manerba is characterized by its rocky walls that drop down into the lake. From the small hamlet of Montinelle we can reach the highest region of the promontory from the top of which it is possible to see the whole of the Garda basin towards the Sirmione peninsular, the characteristic outline of Mt. Baldo and the Pre-Alps that circle the largest of the Italian lakes. The iron *Cross* and the few scanty traces of the

Balbiana: the Church of St. Lucy (above left); the ancient Parish church (above right); the church of St. Mary and detail of a frescoe (adjacent).

Early Mediaeval **Fortress** can be seen in this panoramic spot. When it was besieged by the French, it had already been an integral part of the Longobard defensive system and it managed to resist attack for a long time. It was again witness to many battles during the time of the anti-Brescian rebellions (13th century) and during the times of the bitter strifes between the Guelfi and the Ghibelline during the 13th century. The relentless decay of the impregnable fortress began in the second half of the 16th century, when it was first demolished. The official act of destruction dates back to 1787, when, following the orders of the Venetian superintendent, to eliminate once and for all, the threat constituted by a group of bandits who had found shelter in the fortress, which became the starting point from which they ventured to carry out their criminal deeds.

THE CHURCH OF SANTA LUCIA

In the hamlet of Balbiana stands the church of Santa Lucia (11th century) which has a very simple architectural form, a semi-circular apse and a small tapered bell tower. The interior, consisting of one nave has, on the side of the apse, 16th century frescoes depicting subjects from the Gospels. On the triumphal arch is a painting of the *Annunciation*, whilst Gothic-style frescoes adorn the nave (the *Madonna and Saints*).

THE PARISH CHURCH OF SANTA MARIA

In the hamlet of Pieve Vecchia is situated the Parish Church of Santa Maria, which, despite the alternations to which it has been subjected during the course of the centuries, denotes an 11th century Romanesque structure. On the side of the construction there is a square belltower, built from square stone blocks, and has, on one side, a plaque dating back to the Roman period. The interior of the building, is divided into three aisles, which converge into one central apse, and holds on the site of the apse, a valuable cycle of frescoes of the Rimini school or at least of the Romagna school of the first part of the 16th century. In the hollow of the apse are the *Christ*, *The Symbols of the Evangelists* and *two Angels*. The triumphal arch is decorated with an *Annunciation*. Other pieces of frescoes dating from the 13th century depict a *Mitred Bishop* and figures of *Saints*. The main altar-piece shows a work done by the young G. Andrea Bertanza of Padenghe, portraying the *Virgin with St. Rocco, St. Sebastian, St. Siro and St. Savino* (16th century).

SAN FELICE DEL BENACO

The town is situated in the upper part of the Valténesi, in an almost central position in respect to the promontary, which stretches out over the lake, and separates the gulfs of Salò and Manerba. There have been settlements in the district of San Felice since Prehistoric times, and there are also traces of lake-dwellings and evidence of the Roman period and remains of an ancient necropolis. The landscape of this area is of great value-here we can find the charming towns of Portese and the evocative island of Garda - and moreover it offers impressive panoramic views towards the lower basin of Garda and the picturesque gulfs of Salò and Manerba where the "Fortress" emerging from the lake, irregularly outlines

S. Felice del Benaco: the façade of the Sanctuary of Carmine (above) on the opposite page, detail of a frescoe and "Saints" by the maestro of San Felice (below).

The Island of Garda: a general view (opposite page) and Villa Cavazza (above).

the profile of Dante Alighieri. Of great significance, both artistically and architecturally are the 17th **Town Hall** building, once "The Mountain of Pity", the small **Church of San Fermo** of the 15th century, where one can see a frescoe by Giovanni da Ulma and the 16th century **Parish Church** which has a painting by Romanino portraying the *Madonna in Glory and Saints*, together with paintings by C. Carloni and by Bertanza. But the most interesting element is the **Sanctuary of the Carmelites** which is found at the end of a road which has porphyry paving and which is shaded on both sides by two rows of cypress trees. This valuable construction of Romanesque-Gothic stamp is preceded by a protiro (entrance hall) and also has a beautiful belltower. The interior, which has one central nave is architecturally very interesting because of a series of Gothic arches and a beautiful cycle of 4th - 5th century frescoes, where those done by the famous maestro of San Felice depicting *Saints* and the *Annunciation* stand out.

THE ISLAND OF GARDA

The enchanting island of Garda which is the largest of the lake, rises at a little distance from the small peninsular of San Fermo, flanked by the *Grosti*, picturesque rocks that are dominated by cypresses and a luxuriant vegetation. The island is a private property and therefore cannot be visited and boats are not allowed to land on it. It is possible, however, to navigate around it. The island dominates the romantic Garda landscape because of its fascinating form, shaped by splendid little creeks, and because of its extraordinary colours and its splendid vegetation that covers it and practically hides it from view. A little to the south of the island *the rocks of "Altare"* rise up from the waters of the lake, so-called due to the ancient custom of celebrating mass, once a year, in the presence of fishermen who come from all over the lake and who from their fishing boats, take part in the mass. The island of Garda, which is around one kilometre in length and has an aver-

Above: a view of the gulf of Salò; the promenade and the Cathedral (adjacent).

age width of 60 metres was inhabited by the Romans; in the Early Middle Ages Carlo Magno donated it to the Veronese monks of San Zenone. Later on Federico 1 gave it to Bienio di Manerba. Subsequently it became a den for pirates, who lived all over the Garda basin, it was then chosen by St. Francis as the site for a hermitage, which was built there in the 13th century and for this reason the island of Garda was known as the "Island of Friars". It is almost certain that the island was visited by St. Anthony of Padua and by the poet Alighieri when he was in exile and who was sheltered by the Veronese family, della Scala. In the 15th century St. Bernardino of Siena transformed the building into a convent. Subsequently the island, which had already been the seat of a theology school, passed through the hands of nobles, and then finally came under the control of the Borghese, who comissioned the architect Luigi Revelli, to construct a princely Villa there. The sumptuous building, known today as the **Villa Cavazza**, which gets its name from the present-day owners, is in exquisite Venetian style, and brings to mind the *Ducal Palace*; it was finished in 1901, and has an enormous park in which many specimens of the characteristic flora of Garda can be seen. To the south of the island near the Rocca of Manerba off the shore of the Punta Belvedere rises the *Isle of San Biagio* and the rocks known as *The Rabbits* (i Conigli).

Above: Salò, the façade of the Cathedral; the façade and portal of the Cathedral (adjacent).

SALÒ

The "little Athens" of Garda faces its enchanting gulf, situated in the mid-western part of Garda. The town has a typical lakeside climate which is particularly mild and moderate, for it is protected in the north by the overhanging slopes of Mt. San Bartolomeo which forms an impassable barrier to the cold air currents. Surrounded by verdant sloping hills, with rows of abundant vegetation (mainly Mediterranean) it offers extremely evocative panoramic views over the gulf and on those nearby, which come one after the other along the western part of Garda and towards the distant and haughty mass of Mt. Baldo, often covered with a white mantle of snow. Here the contrasts of light and colour take on an almost quivering and extremely picturesque aspect during the various hours of the day, whilst in the air one can smell the balsamic perfume of the flowers and of the lush vegetation, lulled by the placid and serene movement of the waters of the lake.

The belief that Salò is of Roman origin is backed by numerous and continuous findings which bring to light reminders of the ancient *Salodium* . The place name refers

to a probable deposit of salt present in Roman times. However some hypothesis suggest that the place was one of transit where people from outside Europe passed through on their way towards the Po valley basin or towards the Germanic world. At the turn of the 14th century the place became the chief town of a vast territory known as the *Community* or the *Country of the Riviera* or quite simply as the *Riviera of Salò*. In the 15th century, Beatrice della Scala began the supervising of the restructuring of the mediaeval town walls; then up until 1797, Salò was included amongst the territories administrated by the Serene Republic of Venice. Sripped of its autonomist privileges by Bonaparte it was seriously hit by a violent earthquake which, at the beginning of this century, ruined to a great extent the towns of the lakeside. Salò became the seat of the ephemeral Italian Social Republic, established by Mussolini between 1943 - 1945. Salò and Polpenazze compete for the honour of being the town there Gasparo da Salò, was born. Gasparo da Salò was a famous lute maker and perfectionist of the violin, and his family came from the suburb of the Valténesi. Amongst other illustrious men who were born here, note should be made of Silvan Cattaneo (16th century) the writer, the painter Sante Cattaneo (1739 - 1819), known as "the Saint"; the musician Marco Enrico Bossi (1861 - 1925); the academician Mattia Butturini (1752 - 1817); the painter Angelo Landi (1879 - 1944) and Antonio Scaino, the author of a treatise on a ball game (1524 - 1612).

Adjacent: Salò, the Cathedral, detail of the portal; the interior, the "Deposition" (below); on the opposite page, details of paintings and sculptures to be found in the interior, amongst which can be found the famous golden altar-piece of the XVth century (above right).

THE CATHEDRAL

Amongst the numerous buildings of the town, which are all architecturally and artistically pleasing, the magnificent bulk of the cathedral of Salò stands out, considered one of the most prestigious and excellent religious buildings of the entire territory of Garda. The building, in Gothic-Renaissance style, was begun in 1453, as an epigraph, still legible today, bears witness. The epigraph is on the site of an ancient church, of which only the lower section of the belltower remains. Dedicated to *Mary, Virgin of the Annunciation* it was carried out by Filippo delle Vacche who based it on the Veronese church of *Sant'Anastasia*. Vacche was also in charge of the work done on the cupola, which is in the Venetian Gothic style. The hut-like brick façade is unfinished, and is divided by vertical projections. The remarkable marble doorway shows Renaissance characteristics and catches the eye thanks to the sculptures done by Antonio della Porta and Gasparo da Cairano who were its designers. Above the doorway, crowned by a triangular tympanum, a big "eye" opens in the façade. The immense interior, grandiose and monumental, is divided into three aisles by imposing columns which support the richly decorated arches. The side chapels are a 16th century addition carried out under the orders of San Carlo Borromeo. The interior of the cupola is a masterpiece of geometric architecture with wonderful frescoes depicting the *Four Evangelists* done by Palma the Younger. Amongst the numerous works of art which greatly enrich the artistic content of the interior of Salò Cathedral, the beautiful wooden *Cross* which dominates the presbyterial part, hanging from the gothic vaults is of particular interest. The work, which dates from 1449 was carried out by Giovanni da Ulma, otherwise known as *Johannes teutonichus*. On the main altar, a superb 15th century golden altar piece stands out. This was executed by the engraver Bartolomeo da Isola Dovarese, who was also in charge of the project. The statues, representing *Christ Arisen* (in the upper part) and the *Virgin on the Throne* (lower part) with

a retinue of patron saints of the eight churches, which, in olden days, made up the rectorate of Salò, are all works of the artist Pietro Bussolo of Milano. The magnificent organ dates back to the first half of the 16th century and was carried out by Giovan Giacomo and Gian Francesco Antegnani, both from Brescia. Later (in 1600) Palma the Younger painted the doors. Three other works by the same painter are the *Annunciation* and the *Assunzione della Vergine* and the *Visitation*. Amongst the other paintings in the cathedral are, *St. Anthony of Padua* and the *Madonna and St. Bonaventura and St. Sebastian* by Gerolamo Romanino,; a *Pietà* and a *San Gerolamo* by Zenon Veronese; a polyptych by Paolo Veneziano; *The Virgin*

and Angels and *The Adoration of the Magi* by Andrea Celesti. The *Paradise* by Malosso (G.B. Trotti) can be seen in the chapel of the S.S. Sacrament. Amongst the sculptures, a wooden group of figures depicting the *Deposition* done by an unknown sculptor of the upper Adige region of the 16th century stands out from the rest. The only remaining elements of the 14th century town walls, built by the della Scala family are the two gates, which even today lead to the oldest central parts of the town. The so-called **Fortress Gate** is surmounted by the *Clock Tower*, which is of exquisite architectural workmanship, and rises from the centre of a precious baluster.

The characteristic *Victory Square* looks out onto the

View of the town with the busy lakeside walk and snow-topped mountains in the background.

panoramic and scenographical lakeside; facing it is the **Town Hall Building** marked by an arcade on the ground floor, once a seat of the podestà. The 16th century Renaissance work, was carried out by Sansovino and shows up in the reconstructions that were necessary after the earthquake of 1901. Inside the building a valuable painting, done by the 17th century artist Angelo Bertanza, representing the *Triumph of the Cross* can be seen. There are also frescoes by the local artist Angelo Landi, and a bust of Gaspare of Salò attributed to Angelo Zanelli, inside the cathedral.

Alongside the latter, the **Palace of the Magnifica Patria** (16th century) looks out across the lake. This building used to be the residence of the superintendent of the Riviera of Salò at the time of the domination of the Serene Republic of Venice. Inside can be seen the *Athenaeum of Salò*, established in the 16th century, and the *Museum of the Blue Ribbon*, which contains documents dating back to the time of Bonaparte and keepsakes dating back to the First World War. In the hamlet of Barbarano, near to the coast of Garda, is the 16th century is the **Martinengo Palace**, built by the marquis Sforza-Pallavicino, characterised by its fortified style and a beautiful adjoining park/garden full of water-lilies and flights of steps.

GARDONE RIVIERA

The town, considered to be one of the most precious gems along the spectacular coast nearest to Brescia, looks out on the hydrographical left of the alluvial delta formation determined by the Barbarano torrent, onto the lake, and it stretches, practically continuosly until Fasano. Gardone Riviera has had, even from its etymology, a pleasant climate, which makes it on of the most popular and well-known residential centres of the entire Garda basin. The mild coastal climate, extremely pleasant even during the toughest winter months, makes Gardone Riviera the centre of attraction for a vast clientele, above all for the Germanic races, who like to stay here throughout each season of the year. The first climatic and weather studies carried out in the town west of Garda, date back to 1885 and bear the signature of Dr. Koeniger who, practically paved the way for the ever- increasing tourist renown which the place now enjoys. Among the features which compete in determining the conditions of such a pleasant climate, mention should be made, above all, to its marvellous geografical position, picturesquely looking out over the lake, along a sickleshaped bay opposite the evocative island of Garda, and it is sheltered in the north by the fortified walls of the Pizzocolo and Spino moun-

tains, which prevent the entry of cold northern currents. Therefore the florid and fertile Mediterranean vegetation thrives here, which in fact, extends up to a height of 300 metres, covering the terraced slopes, the hills and valleys that surround the town. In this triumph of green chromatic tonality, we find, here and there, plants typical to the Garda area: olives and laurels with, naturally, the noble figures of the cypress trees. All this, gives Garda the aspect of a town which is perennially subjected to the Spring winds, giving the scenic villas and pretty residences, which form a part of this "paradise" landscape, an even greater emphasis of beauty. Fasano was already established in the Roman age, and was one of the first inhabited places of the district. Evidence dating back to the 8th century has shown that there was a Longobard nucleus set in Gardone. The town soon became a "feud" of the Bishop's Palace of Brescia, forming, from the 16th century onwards, an integral part of that "Magnificent Country" which appealed to the Venetians, invoking protection against the expansionist intentions of the Visconti family of Milan. Following the Diet of Worms (1521) the town became one of the territories controlled by Venice, remaining faithful to the insignia of Leone Marciano, until the fall of that powerful maritime (lagoon) town (1797). At Gardone di Sopra we find the **Church of San Nicola**, which dominates a beautiful small piazza from the top of a fortified structure. The elegant

Gardone Riviera: the promenade and the river basin (on the opposite page); hotels and residences along the promenade (above).

49

Gardone Riviera: a view from one of the tourist boats and the Grand Hotel (opposite page); the Parish Church of St. Nicola at Gardone di sopra (above left); the Tower of San Marco (above right); the Mausoleum of the Vittoriale (adjacent).

18th century building was built on the site of an old church, by the architect Paolo Soratini of Lonato. The beautiful façade of two orders depicts neo-Classical themes and is flanked by a slender Romanesque bell-tower. The interio, in the Baroque style has a painting by Zenon Veronese depicting the *Descent of the Holy Spirit*, while the choir stalls have an altar-piece, painted by Palma the Younger. An element of particular artistic value is the silver frame of the altar of the Madonna, carried out by the artists of Brescia in the 18th century. Another outstanding building is the **Tower of Saint Mark**, once known as the *Ruhland Tower* and then transformed by D'Annunzio who made a dock from which he used to leave by motorboat for his trips around the lake. The tower, which is reflected in the waters of the lake, is surrounded by a verdant park. The sumptuous **Villa Alba** is a marvellous testimony of neoclassical architecture; it has an elegant colonnaded façade, surmounted by an elaborate triangular tympanum. Today it is used as a congress centre, surrounded by a large, luxurious park. Other monuments of interest are the Romanesque **Church of St. Anthony the Abbot** at Morgnaga, the 17th century **Church of St. Faustino** at Fasano and the **Hruska Botanical Gardens**, begun in 1910, by the professor who gave his name to the gardens, and who collected various specimens of Mediterranean, Alpine and African fauna, using unusual and ingenious artificial methods to re-create a place where various specimens could thrive.

IL VITTORIALE

This scenic complex, deeply emersed with recollections and mementoes of D'Annunzio, is set in Gardone di Sopra, on a panoramic hill, rendered even more evocative by the extensive line of cypress trees that emerge from the large woods of olive, and oleander trees. In this enviroment, where the panorama extends towards the Garda basin well beyond the curious outline of the Manerba promontory, until the Sirmione peninsula and gradually up to the Veronese bank with Garda, the Punta San Vigilio and Malcesine, picturesquely set at the foot of Mount Baldo, there was once the *Villa Cargnacco*.

The Villa was little more than a farm holding, a simple unpretentious building, set on the slopes along the coast near the tumultuous flow of the Rio Torto. This decidedly idyllic and fascinating setting, coloured by a luxuriant Mediterranian vegetation, which together with the arboreous species already mentioned, and the presence of myrtle, laurel, wisteria, palm trees and roses, all played a part in seducing the soul of Gabriele D'Annunzio, who had stayed here, and who bought the building in February 1921. The bard of Pescara, entrusted the brothers Giancarlo and Ruggero Maroni with the work of transforming this modest hillside building into one of the most magnificent residences of the entire territory of Garda, not devoid of splendid decorations and redundant rhetoric which contributed a characterstic element of that mystic, sensual, heroic, and yet histrionic personality of the illustrious man of letters living in the Abruzzi.

Visits to the various surroundings of the Vittoriale are made by crossing the market routes, which make up an unusual labyrinth; a kaleidescope of lanes, open spaces, flights of steps and slopes, always in harmony with a particularly vivid and generous Nature, which here and there allows enchanting glimpses of the sky-blue lake and the green hills that fade into the intense azzurre of the sky.

Just beyond the entrance, a sequence of arches defines the lane, in the middle of which stands the unusual structure named *Pilo del Piave*, surmounted by a clay figuration of *Vittoria* by A. Minerbi. A little further ahead, on the right, we come to an extremely panoramic place - the suggestive **Teatro all'Aperto** (open air theatre). This architectural structure re-echoes the theatrical models of Classicism; in its simplicity of statement and in its essentiality of form it is however blessed with enviable accoustics. For this reason, it is still used on hot, luminous summer nights, for staging theatrical representations of outstanding cultural content, and often presents famous pieces from the vast repertoir of D'Annunzio. Down below, beyond the tops of the cypresses and other trees we can make out the profile of the coast of Garda, and on a particularly clear day one can see far into the distance, taking in the magnificent panorama.

One now reaches the so-called *piazzetta Dalmata* on which stands the homonymous *Pilo*. The buildings named *Prioria* and *Schifamondo* look out onto the piazza. The front of the **Prioria** is decorated with numerous

Above: the entrance to the Vittoriale; on the opposite page the façade and portico of the Schifamondo (the Loathing of the World) (above); a view of the Mausoleum; the façade of the Priory.

coats of arms and one enters it through an elaborate doorway supported by columns. The building is the place where D'Annunzio lived until his death on 1st March 1938. The interior of the building holds an unusual collection of furniture, furnishings and objects, where various styles are blended and imposed one on the other, bringing together elements of diverse origins, where we can only catch faint glimpses of the complex personality of D'Annunzio who appears to have enjoyed creating his own personalised world, leaving the task of perpetuating the myth of his literary vicissitudes and his soldier-like exploits to his antiques, souvernis and momentoes.

The Music Room, also known and the *Counterpoint Room*, is dedicated to Gasparo da Salò, universally believed to be the perfectionist, if not the inventor, of the violin. The room was designed as a place for putting on the concerts of the "Vittoriale Quartet"; lit by unusual lamps (in the form of pumpkins) and decorated with dark-red brocade and black lamé it contains many objects and unusual knick-knacks such as a Buddha, a sculptural effigy of Diana the Huntress and a work of sculpture depicting Leda and the swan.

The Globe Room contains the most significant part of the so-called Thode library, an organ, some Napoleonic souvernis and an Austiran rifle, while on the table in the hall is the globe which gives its name to the room.

The Zambracca room acted as a kind of antechamber for the bedrooms, and at the same time was used as a

The Vittoriale: the interiors of the Priory, the Globe Room (above); one of the bedrooms (below).

small study and a dressing room. In the middle of the room is the table on which the most treasured possessions of D'Annunzio are still to be seen and where the poet used to write and eat. It was at this same table that D'Annunzio died (from an embolism). In the solid walnut wardrobe are the clothes that give us a glimpse of D'Annunzio's eccentric personality, and which also provide a significant and interesting element in this highly original microcosm of D'Annunzio.

Leda's Room has a decidedly oriental atmosphere, and holds numerous objects and treasures, wall plates, cushions and rugs. Next to the bedroom, described above, are the *Veranda di Apollino* and the *Blue Bathroom*, so-called because of the predominance of that colour; this is a room full of objects amongst which many Persian tiles catch the eye.

The Leper's Room is inspired by the concept of death, and is characterised by a bed used by the poet himself, which resembles a coffin.

The Relics'Room testifies in an irreproachable manner, the message which D'Annunzio wanted to make, leaving this task to the diverse objects and possessions which come from such unusual sources.

The Lyre Room (Cheli) owes its perculiar name to a huge turtel whose shell was used as a model for the bronze sculpture on the table, done by Renato Brozzi in 1928. This room, which used to be a dining room, has a markedly decadent atmosphere. The walls, of wood panelling, are painted in dramatic colours such as black, azzurre, red and gold.

*The Vittoriale: the interiors of the Priory,
the Lute Room (above);
the Music Room (below).*

The Vittoriale: the Open-Air Theatre (above); the Tomb of
G. D'Annunzio and the tombs of the Fallen (adjacent); on the
opposite page, the S.S. "Puglia" and the view towards the lake:
the figure-head depicting the "Vittoria Alata"; the S.S. Puglia on
the late poet's estate.

The Oratorio Dalmata was the room where the poet received his visitors - amongst whom also Benito Mussolini
came to pay homage to D'Annunzio, in his unusual
house, in May 1925. The room was lit up by candlelight
and pervaded by the acute perfume of incense. In the
Oratorio Dalmato are many antiques and momentoes; the
most eye-catching object, which hangs from the ceiling is
the propeller of the seaplane, used by Francesco de Pine-
do, to carry out the historic flight in stages from Sesto
Calende to Melbourne.
The so-called *Officina* was used as a study in which
D'Annunzio used to work; to enter this room the visitor
must stoop, as the door is much lower than a normal one;
a latin motto is printed on the architrave and everything
here seems to evoke an almost sacred atmosphere. The
furnishings of the room, decidedly more staid and mea-
sured than the other rooms, seem to be characterised by
a bronze sculpture depicting *Eleonora Duse*, done by Ar-
rigo Minerbi, which the poet liked to have behind him,
while he worked. The myth of this theatrical actress from
Vigevano (who was sentimentally linked with D'Annunzio for a long time) lingers imperceptible but constantly
throughout this unusual residence.

On the first floor is another smaller studio known as *The Studio of the Maimed*. The reason for the room's strange name comes from the fact that here, among furniture brought from the poet's previous home, D'Annunzio used to deal with his correspondence. Because of the impossible task of replying personally to all the letters he received daily, D'Annunzio hung a drawing of a hand with the inscription *Recisa quiescit* on the door.

Lo **Schifamondo** (the Loathing of the World) owes its original name to the fact that is was here that D'Annunzio used to isolate himself, constructing a physical and spiritual barrier between himself and the world he detested and abhorred. Today it has become a museum and it also contains the *Auditorium* where concerts and cultural activities are held; from its cupola hangs the *Aeroplane SVA*, which D'Annunzio used to complete the leggendary (propagandistic) air-raid on Vienna on August 9th 1918. In the porch of the Schifamondo - equipped with interesting archives and an extensive library, drawings in the style of Michelangelo, letters and writings in the poet's own hand, and an exhibition of his works and momentoes connected with Eleonora Duse - is the *FIAT 4 Pininfarina* with which D'Annunzio travelled, in 1919, from Ronchi to Fiume.

Outside the museum buildings, a small alley that winds along the thick vegetation of the hills, leads us to one of the most emblematic and characteristic spots of the D'Annunzio itinerary: here, set in the hillside, emerging from the line of cypress trees, stands the **Nave Puglia** (ship) with its prow decorated by a bronze figure-head depicting the *Winged Victory* which looks down on the Lake of Garda.

The lake seems like a surreal image, emersed in a decidedly dream-like atmosphere. The prow of the ship is one of the most significant panoramic observation posts of the whole Vittoriale complex, due to its unusual and remarkable setting and it never ceases to amaze the many groups of tourists who come here.

In the vicinity stands the *Fountain of the Dolphin* which gets its water from the water course of the Rio Torto; rebaptised *Acqua Pazza* (Mad Water) by D'Annunzio. Not far away there is also the long, low building which, characterised by the inscription *Memento audere semper* holds the **MAS** (antisubmarine craft). It was in this craft that the poet led the so-called "Beffa di Buccari" (the Buccari hoax) in February 1918, which culminated in the sinking of the warship Santo Stefano by a flottila commanded by the Lieutenant of the vessel, Luigi Rizzo.

On the summit of a neighbouring hill, in a beautiful scenic spot, is the **Mausoleo** (Mausoleum); the grandiose funeral building in a circular shape. Of special interest are the internal passage-ways and the external concentric passages which encircle the centre of the building. On the top of the monumental sanctuary, above an elevated pedestal, built of enormous square blocks, is set the ark inside which were placed the mortal remains of D'Annunzio in 1963. All around, arranged in circles, are the arks containing the mortal remains of ten soldiers who were D'Annunzio's war companions.

On the opposite page: the Vittoriale; the Aeroplane SVA (above); the anti-submarine apparatus (below); Gardone Riviera, the Hruska Botanical Gardens and floral species (above).

59

FASANO

The enchanting coastal town of Fasano was formed by the separation of the centres of Fasano di Sopra and Fasano di Sotto and is included in the administrative limits of the Comune of Gardone Riviera. The lower part of the town is spread out along an outstretched promontory towards the waters of the lake. Being a health resort and also a popular residential spot, it is full of charming villas and splendid residences which are dotted here and there amongst the thick green surroundings. Among the numerous villas, special mention should be made of the **Villa Ideale**, where Mussolini's personal doctor stayed, at the time of the Social Republic; the **Villa Cristofori**, once the residence of the German Ambassador; and the villa, in the town of Bornico where the statesman, Giuseppe Zanardelli lived up until his death. Inside the **Church of S. Faustino** (17th century) is a painting by C. Ballini, depicting *Christ between SS. Faustino e Giovita*.

MADERNO

This pretty costal town in the vicinity of Brescia looks out onto an idyllic gulf, and its boundaries are defined by the promontory of the same name and by the evocative Punta di Fasano. The houses are arranged along the southern part of the alluvial promontory formed by deposits transported by the river Toscolano, beyond which stands the town bearing the same name. Toscolano together with Maderno, form one single administrative entity. Blessed with a pleasant lakeside climate, and protected in the north by elevated mountain slopes, it is counted as being one of the most temperate health resorts throughout each

season of the year, and consequently it is a much sought-after spot and frequented by vast international clientele. Here the rich and flourishing Mediterranean vegetation is further enriched by species such as lemons and oranges which blend pleasantly with the oleanders, the palm trees and the olives enriching the coastal front and covering the entire promontory, as well as the initial buttresses of the mountainous slopes, cut by the small valleys along which run pleasant and delight fulstreams. The town is linked to Torri del Benaco by a ferry. In the Communal Age Maderno was the main town of the Riviera Bresciana, being in high favour with Federico I (Barbarossa/Red Beard), but it was also without doubt an extremely important town even in Roman times. Its importance gradually diminished in the second half of the 14th century when Beatrice Della Scala made the neighbouring Salò the capital of the Magnifica Patria. At the time of the domination of the Serene Venetian Republic, it continued to benefit from its ancient autonomous prerogatives.

The Church of St. Andrea is a valuable Romanesque-Lombardic jewel, built in the 12th century, on the ruins of a paleochristian temple. The beautiful façade consists of chromatism determined by the use of several different types of stone, among which the famous Veronese red. The architecture recalls to mind elements which existed in San Zeno Veronese, whilst the large abundance of sculptures in the magnificent porch imitates the work of the Lombardic skilled workers, who interpreted the themes

Toscolano: the Parish Church (above); detail of the portal (adjacent); on the opposite page, Toscolano, a panoramic view and the port.

that were dear to the figurative Christian tradition. Some material, taken from Roman buildings, show richly-decorated bas-reliefs. The interior, divided into 3 aisles, contains an altarpiece by A. Paglia depicting *Saints Filippo Neri, Carlo Borromeo, Gaetano and Giuseppe*: a 10th century painting by Andrea Bertanza (*San Lorenzo Martyr*); a 17th century painting depicting *the Baptism of Christ*; 15th century affrescoes and an organ dating back to the second half of the 16th century. Other tourist attractions are the **Church of S. Ercolano** (19th century) which contains beautiful pictures and the relics of the patron saint, transferred to this church from the crypt of S. Andrea; the **Church of S. Bartolomeo** (*Sacred Family* by Palma the Younger) and the **Monument to Giuseppe Zanardelli** (L. Bistolfi).

TOSCOLANO

Crossing the river, which bears the same name, and which further along can also be crossed by a 14th century *bridge* built by hand and consisting of one span, one reaches Toscolano, set in the upper region of the promontory which it shares with Maderno. It is believed that the town was founded by the Etruscans, as several place-names of the district would testify. However it is almost certain that Toscolano was once know as *Benacum* in Roman times and that since then, the name encompasses the whole of the lakeside basin. From Roman times the

remains of a villa believed to be contemporary to that of Desenzano still exist, and here we can see important remains of mosaic floors; documentation and evidence of old buildings and pagan temples. In the so-called "Valle delle Cartiere" (beginning from the 14th century) were several factories which produced paper, appreciated everywhere for its excellent quality. In the 15th century the printer, Gabriele di Pietro from Treviso printed some excellent works. Even today the paper mills still exist, even though they have undergone unavoidable transofrmations. The **Church of Saints Peter and Paul** has an adjoining belltower on which there is a plaque, dedicated to Marc'Aurelio by the inhabitants of the town. In the church, built in the second half of the 16th century, one can admire a series of excellent paintings by Andrea Celesti. The **Sanctuary of the Madonna of Benaco** is situated on the site of an ancient pagan temple, of the 1st century B.C. dedicated to Giove Ammone, of which some columns are still to be seen near the steps of the sanctuary. During the first half of the 1950's, following some restoration work, the remains of several beautiful frescoes came to light. Near the ancient port stands the 17th century **Mafizzoli Palace** (once known as *Palace Delay*) which still shows the original 17th century structure and contains many paintings by Andrea Celesti.

Above: Bogliaco, the Church of St. Pier d'Agrino; on the opposite page, Palace of Bettoni (above) and the Italian gardens.

BOGLIACO

This hamlet, in the southern part of the Comune di Gargano, picturesquely looks out onto the western part of Lake Garda and is famous for the superb **Bettoni Palace**, a scenographical 18th century residence, built on the lines of a plan by the Veronese architect Adriano Cristofali. The two marvellous fronts (one facing the lake, and one facing the western part of Garda) catch the eye, because of the pilaster-strips that vertically scan the building and because of the beautiful windows which are surmounted by tympanium, sometimes triangular, sometimes semi-circular; the upper balustrade is defined by a beautiful balcony full of statues. The huge internal rooms contain remarkable paintings by Celesti, Reni, Pitocchetto (Giacomo Cerutti) and by Brusasorci. Beyond the Garda area we find the **Italian Gardens**, connected to the Palazzo by two bridges. The layout of the gardens was designed by the Tuscan Amerigo Vincenzo Pierallini in the second half of the 18th century. Pierallini worked extensively in the Fiorentine district where he designed numerous parks and villa gardens. The gardens are full of rococo elements, water lilies and sculptures by Cignaroli. The 16th century **Church of S. Pier d'Agrino** is preceded by a hallway sustained by columns and flanked by a battlemented bell-tower. The interior, with 3 aisles each separated by columns, contains a wooden statue of exquisite workmanship depicting the patron saint.

GARGNANO

Proceeding up the west coast of Garda towards Riva del Garda Gargnano is situated at a point where the lake is now quite narrow and is dominated by the impending and steep cliffs of the Pre-Alps of Brescia. However the lemon groves and the fertile vegetations suggest a mild, gentle climate which make it an esteemed health-resort. Ancient plaques, dating from the Roman Age, indicate that the place dates from at least the 3rd century B.C. Already cited as *Garniano* up until the 11th century, it acquired its present name at the start of the 13th century. Subjected to the rule of Castelbarco in the first half of the 14th century it later became the possession of the Milanese Visconti family, before passing under the control of Venice (15th century). The town is equipped with a pretty little port which welcomes tourist boats; tourism, has in fact taken the place of the traditional fishing activities.

In Gargnano there are the two **Feltrinelli Villas**; the first, in the town of San Faustino, looks out picturesquely onto the lake; it dates back to the end of the last century and Mussolini stayed here at the time of the Social Republic. The second villa, contemporary with the first, was designed by the architect Solmi. It was the residence of the

Above: Gargnano, a panoramic view; Gargnano, a view of the town and the promenade (adjacent); on the opposite page, Gargnano as seen from the Gardesana.

secretary of the so-called Republic of Salò and nowadays it acts as a centre for Italian language courses for foreigners from the University of Milan.

On the shores of the lake, at the foot of the precipitious walls of the "Cima Comer" stands, in an extremely pleasant atmosphere, near the old extensive lemon groves, the **Small Church of S. Giacomo de Calì**. This is one of the oldest places of worship in the western area of Garda; the small Romanesque building dates back to the 12th century and its antique origins are also confirmed by a well-known popular dialectal saying. The façade built from blocks of irregular stones, is surmounted by a beautiful bell-tower. On the outside, along one side of the church, some 14th century frescoes are still legible, depicting *S. Anthony the Abbot, between St. Paul and an evangelist, St. Anthony of Padua and St. Christopher with Child*. The interior contains frescoes dating back to the same time as a wooden sculpture depicting the patron saint (16th century). The **Church of S. Francesco**, dating from the second half of the 13th century seems to date back to a Francescan hermitage established on the bankside of Lake Garda by the great man of Assisi himself (San Francesco). The simple hut-like façade is vertically divided by pilaster strips and is further enriched by a beautiful doorway. In a niche is a sulptural representation of *S. Antonio* (14th century). The interior, now reconverted into a single nave, contains a 16th century painting by Andrea Bertanza depicting *San Stefano Martyr* and other paintings, contemporary with the Lombardic artists. On the northern side of the building we can see a sculptural representation of the *Miracle of the Stigmata* and, interesting frescoes dating from the 13th - 14th

On the opposite page: Gargnano, the promenade and the Villa Feltrinelli (below); the Church of St. Giacomo de Cali (adjacent) and external frescoes (below).

On the opposite page: Gargnano, the Church and Cloisters of St. Francis; a panoramic view towards Mt. Baldo (above); a characteristic lemon-grove on the Gardesana (adjacent).

centuries have been discovered inside the bell-tower. Between the sacristy and the cloister is a remarkable portal in black marble with high-reliefs of religious subjects. The **Cloister** has considerable environmental merits and its sequence of arches, several of which are imprinted with curious and unusual forms, typical of Moorish architecture, catch the eye. The capitals of the columns, decorated with fruits and orange and lemon leaves seem to enhance the tradition that likes to see the cultivation of these citrus fruits introduced in the Garda area by the Francescans.

The **Church of San Martino**, restructured in the 14th century and built by Rodolfo Vantini of Brescia; its origins go back to the 11th century. Its façade is endowed with a magnificent colonnaded pronaos; the interior consisting of just one aisle, contains a painting of the *Last Supper* carried out in the manner of the Venetial School of the 17th century, and is believed by some people to originate from the workshop of Veronese.

In the vicinity of Villa di Gargnano is situated the **Church of San Tommaso Apostolo**; its interior contains some valuable works of art, including a wooden statue depicting *S. Carlo Borromeo*, and a fresco dating back to the 16th century depicting *S. Libera*, the protectress of women giving birth. This church is set in a pleasant and panoramic landscape; from the small piazza in front of the building one has a marvellous view over Gargnano and the lake.

TIGNALE

The scattared hamlets of the Comune of Tignale stretch out along a false plain which dominates the western part of Garda and are characterised by environmental and panoramic merits of a sublime level. The characteristics of the landscape are stamped by a morphology which at various intervals becomes softer but ofter includes steep cliffs and precipitous walls, often marked by picturesque waterfalls. Woodland patches are alternated by the cultivation of trees, predominantly those of the olive, and fruit trees, while towards the lake we get spectacular panoramic glimpses of the higher part of the basin, enclosed between elevated mountain peaks ranging also to

On the opposite page: the Western part of the Gardesana (above); a view of the Garda basin with the Sanctuary of the Madonna of Monte Castello (below), the façade of the Sanctuary (above).

On the following pages: aspects of the Western part of Garda (left) and the background of Monte Baldo (right).

the lowest part, marked by the idyllic gulfs and pleasant peninsulas that act as a background to the undulating gentle Morainic slopes of the amphitheatre of the Garda area.

Already established by the Galli Cenomani since the 5th century B.C. the land was dependent on the *Municipium* of Brescia in Roman times. During the reign of the Della Scala family the Veronese lords built a fortified structure; afterwards the town was ruled by the Visconti family of the Episcopacy of Trento and of the Serene Republic.

 The most important tourist attraction is the **Sanctuary of the Madonna of Monte Castello**; also known as *Castellana del Garda* the evocative building is set in an extremely scenographic spot, on the summit of a hill, whose southern walls fall vertically to the lake. All around, a panorama of indescribable beauty stretches out; the origins of this building seem to date back to the 9th century, but it appears that an ancient temple structure already existed on the site. In the Middle Ages a fortress was built which was then later converted for sacred purposes. Amongst the works of art, worthy of mention are the paintings of Palma the Younger, Alessandro Campi, a fresco in the Gothic style and frescoes of the 14th century Veronese school.

GARDESANA OCCIDENTALE

This road, together with the one bearing the same name that runs along the western edge of the Garda basin, was constructed and opened to motor traffic in the 1920's and the first years of the 1930's. Its layout, chiefly in the upper part of the Lake of Garda, shows aspects of marked landscape suggestions which blend admirably with the bold architecture (bridges, tunnels) and other works carried out by Man, which overcome the natural ruggedness of the land. The road runs at intervals above and alongside the lake, allowing panoramic glimpses of great effect, towards the Veronese banks, surmounted by the impending and often snow-covered profile of Mt. Baldo, or towards the northern top of Garda, marked by the unmistakable profile of Mt. Brione. From time to time long tunnels allow one to pass through the rock walls which, in this area, fall ruggedly down to the edge of the lake. Here and there, the road runs through impervious gorges, on which the precipitous rocks and craggy rock-walls seem to swoop down, whilst elsewhere the road passes through steep and suggestive ravines, softened by the serene beauty of the lake. The progress of the Gardesana, which is extremely tortuous and curvilinear, is marked by the green outlines of the cypress trees which line the road, acting as a natural guard-rail.

On the opposite page, the harsh morphology of the western part of the Gardenese; the plateau of Tignale and the upper basin of Garda (above); the rocky walls which dominate the Gardesana (adjacent).

TREMOSINE

The scattered hamlets of Tremosine are set along what is wrongly defined as a plateau; in reality this is a false plain which, as in the case of Tignale, presents aspects of extremely scenic and environmental suggestions. The chief town of the Comune is situated at Pieve, a pretty hamlet spread out in the green woods and large meadows which make up a magnificent natural curtain for the beautiful mirror-like lake, the impending mountains and the opposite western part of Garda, where the small pretty town of Malcesine is set. The place was in all probability an ancient Etruscan settlement. This affermation is backed up by the so-called *lapide di Voltino* (Voltino's plaque) which nowadays can be seen in the Roman museum at Brescia. The plaque created problems of language interpretation which have seriously embarrased qualified men of learning and even illustrious historians; on it are written epigraphs in Latin, Etruscan or probably in the language of the ''Cenomani Gauls'', and these are still legible today. Afterwards the town was inhabited by the Galli Cenomani, and by the Romans. In Medieval times there was a castle, the ruins of which can barely be made out. Today Tremosine shares, together with the neighbouring Tignale, the advantages of a pleasant climate, the effects of which can be enjoyed even as far as half-way up the coast. For this reason it is a much frequented and desired spot with holiday makers and tourists in search of tranquility and rest.

At Pieve the interesting **Church of St. John the Baptist** is situated; the church owes its present aspect to works carried out during the 15th century on an old parish church of the 6th century restructured in the 17th century. The simple façade culminating in a tympanum, si scanned by parastrades, whilst the bell-tower imitates the outlines of Romanesque Lombardi styles. The interior, in pure baroque forms is adorned with a remarkable 18th century organ built by the Serassi of Bergamo, with exquisite contemporary wooden engravings done by Giacomo Lucchini of Condino which enrich the choir-stalls and the sacristy furniture, and with frescoes and beautiful paintings. In the adjacent *Parochial House* a valuable architectural particular consisting of a gothic-capital which dates back to the first half of the 15th century can be seen.

Near the church there is a spectacular scenic spot from which one can look out across an evocative yet harsh and wild panorama. A particularly picturesque itinerary goes from the ancient port on the lake to Pieve, running along the inaccessible gorge of Brasa at whose mouth is situated a waterfall. Due to its extraordinary scenic and panoramic characteristic the false plain of Tremosine is also known as *The Garda Balcony*. The whole territory is of extreme naturalistic and geological interest; in the town of Pregasio in the vicinity of the *Church of St. Mark*, some morphological aspects relating back to the ancient Alpine corrugation can still be seen.

On the opposite page: Tremosine, the Parish Church of St. John the Baptist at Pieve (above), the interior and the wooden choir stalls/pews (below right); Tremosine, a view towards Pieve and detail of the town (above).

LIMONE SUL GARDA

A charming tourist resort at the upper western end of Garda, Limone sul Garda stretches out along the narrow strip of land between the waters of the lake and the imposing mountain wall which, in this spot take on the traits of the Dolomitic rock. The town is renowned as being one of the most splendid parts of the upper Garda basin, and owes its fortune and its mythical properties to the extraordinary scenic, environmental and panoramic values which here harmonize and blend indissolubly with the characteristics of the so-called "Olive climate". It is an exceedingly difficult task to put into words the exact dimensions of the landscape and the environment of Limone which are distilled in the intensive azzure of the waters of the lake, in the identical tonality of a sky which is almost always serene and exceptionally clear, and in the enchanting profile of Garda, which from here seems to shed the features of a lake and take on the evocative dimensions of a nordic fiord. All these elements have, throughout history, attracted literary men and men of culture, who at Limone all drew inspiration and obtained material for their work; for example Goethe, Ibsen and D.H. Lawrence. Limone sul Garda is a well-equipped

and hospitable health resort; the natural cordiality and the proverbial kindness of its inhabitants give an ulterior motive for choosing it as a tourist spot. The mild coastal climate, whose beneficial effects can be enjoyed as far up as the northernmost part of the lake, is particularly favourable and inviting here, above all for the numerouse tourists from Central Europe who literally throng the town, as if taking possession of a forbidden fruit. The luxuriant and flourishing Mediterranean vegetation reaches even up to these latitudes and give us species that are quite unusual for these parts, such as palm trees, cedars, olives, coppice woods and naturally lemons.
Lemons were introduced to this area by the Francescan monks who had already set out the first lemon groves at Gargnano. Starting from the 13th century the cultivation of this fruit became a marked characteristic element of the coastal landscape; it is believed that already during the 14th century the lemon groves spread from Gargnano

*The Western Gardesana seen from Limone sul Garda (above);
on the opposite page, a view of Limone sul Garda and its famous
lemon groves.*

Three attractive views over the town.

to Limone and constituted the fulcrum of an anbundant production, destined chiefly for the central European markets. In the Austrian capital people used often to consume large quantities of syrups and distilled drinks obtained from the lemons of the Garda region. Those who wish to think there is a simple etymological connection between the town and the plant itself would be very much mistaken. It is believed, in fact, that Limone is derived from the Latin word *limen* which means "boundary" or "border". The fact that Limone is a boundary territory goes without saying; even today a little way north of the town runs the boundary between the provinces of Brescia and Trento, and the controversies for the possession of the lakeside village between the Lombards and the people of Trento date back as far as the 13th century when Brescia had to use armed resistance to defend its territorial sovereignty which was put under threat by the counts of Arco. As far back as the 14th cent. Limone became famous for its central fishing industries, and fishing, especially for large carps, made up one of the primary activities of its inhabitants, who continued these activites until around 10 years ago before becoming involved with the tourist industry on a large scale. In fairly recent times (at the end of April/beginning of May 1985) an international medical-scientific congress, held in the lakeside town came to surprising conclusions on the im-

pact of the posizion and the climate of Limone on the human organism. The slogan "At Limone You Live Longer" seems to be backed by medical/scientific research, which has discovered a protein in the blood of some of the residents that has beneficial effects for the prevention of sclerosis and heart-attacks. Amongst the most illustrious "sons" of Limone mention should be made of Daniele Comboni, a missionary in Africa during the last century, and the founder of the Sons of the Sacred Heart and of the Sisters of Nigrizia.

The ancient centre of Limone sul Garda slopes down from the lemon groves to the beautiful lakeside and one can discover narrow lanes and extremely characteristic corners, one of these being the cosy little port where the tourist boats and the characteristic fishing boats are moored. The 17th century **Church of St. Benedetto** contains an altarpiece by a Dutch artist of the 16th century; two pictures by Andrea Celesti depicting *The Adoration of the Magi* and the *Supper of Levi* and *Virgin delle Grazie*, an exquisite wooden sculpture. There are many villas and residencies built in the Venetial style which brighten up and enrich the urban landscape. Finally mention should also be made of the little 14th century church of **St. Rocco** in which there is an 18th century altarpiece attributed to N. Grisiani.

Limone sul Garda: lemon stores on the lake (left); the basin (below); next page, views of Limone sul Garda, the lakeside walk, interesting little lanes (above and below left), and the Church of St. Rocco (below right).

RIVA DEL GARDA

Evocatively facing the northern top of the Lake of Garda which here is wedged like a narrow fiord between the Pre-Alps of Brescia and Trentino and the outstretching mountainous formations of Baldo-Monte Altissimo di Nago, Riva del Garda is set in the southernmost part of the low valley of Sarca. Its urbanistic aspect is that of a typical centre which has now acquired town-like dimensions whilst administratively it has the role of the chief town of the Trentine territorial limits which look out over the largest of the Italian lakes. Its geographical position places it in a position of absolute privilege, at the junction with the western and eastern roads going towards the valle dell'Adige (Vallagarina) and going towards the Valle di Ledro which establishes the connection with the valley along which the Chiese river runs.

The scenic landscape of Riva del Garda is marked by the rocky buttresses of the "Rocchetta" which dominates the area in the west and the unusual outline of the Brione mountain, which separates it (it is like a huge boulder facing the shores of the lake) from the mouth of the Sarca which here infuses the waters with those of Garda, making up the chief tributary. All around rise up summits of pure Pre-Alpine character which represent an almost tangible "trait d'union" with the legendary and fairy-like world of the Trentine Dolomites, only a few kilometres away. Looking out and admiring the placid mirror of Lake Garda one can also see on the left the view and the long outline of Mt. Baldo range which comprises in the foreground the high summit of Mt. Altissimo di Nago which makes up its northernmost ramification. The town holds environmental and scenic characteristics which are exceedingly unusual and in a certain sense antithetical: the landscape and nature of these places contain decidedly alpine connotations, while the mildness of the climate and the extraordinary lush vegetation are typical of mediterranean lands. In spite of the latitude, decidedly northern, the climate of Riva is extremely moderate and agreeable throughout each season of the year, and especially during the months traditionally held as being climatically

On the opposite page: the Western part of Garda and the road to Ponale, in the background, Riva del Garda; a view of Riva del Garda (above).

Riva del Garda: panoramica from Bastione (adjacent); the Tower of Apponale and the Third of November Square (below); on the opposite page, a view of the port (above) and the Third of November Square (below).

most severe. Due to this bizarre and pleasant anomaly, which is verified everywhere along the edge of Benaco (Garda), Riva del Garda is rightly considered as being one of the most famous and well-equipped holiday and health resorts. The German speaking people in particular have elected this part of the Trentine coast as an almost obligatory spot for their holidays and weekend outings. It is almost impossible to count, during the weekends, the Tyrolese and Bavaria cars that travel along the Brennero motorway, heading for this part of the Mediterranean that is almost on their own doorstep. If, on one hand, famous men such as Goethe, Nietzche or Mann have admired and extolled the glories of this changeable lake, which often transforms itself into a sea, on the other hand it has been literally invaded by the Germans, the Austrians, the Swiss and the Dutch who rediscover the tranquility and serenity of which mention is made in the pages of the great writers. And when the vigorous breezes of the lake fill the sails of the surfers and the sailing enthusiasts, on land one can admire the mirror-like lake which is a more intense azzurre then the sky above it, while in the clear and limpid air linger the perfumes of the vegetation which includes palms and olive trees, vines and agaves, oleanders and many other species.

The history of the town has its roots planted in Roman times, when it was part of a *vicus* dependent on Brescia, giving hospitality to a college of helmsmen who administered the entire lakeside basin. The first mention of the place in the early Middle Ages, dates back to an Ottonian diploma during the time of the *curtis regia* governed by the Veronese episcopacy. Subsequently it came under the

Adjacent: Riva del Garda, Market Square the town centre (below).

*Riva del Garda: a view of the Fortress and of the promenade (above);
the river basin in the background of the Fortress (adjacent).*

dependence of the episcopal principality of Trentino
(11th century) and here prospered from the point of view
of trade and commerce, becoming an important seat for
fairs and markets. Beginning with the 14th century it fell
to the Veronese Della Scala family, the Milanese Visconti
family and finally came under the control of the Republic
of San Marco, remaining so until the beginning of the
16th century. At first it was occupied by the French, then
at the beginning of the 18th century it was defeated by
Bonaparte, therefore becoming part of Bavaria, of the
Italian Kingdom, of the Austro-Hungarian empire and
finally becoming an integral part of the Italian State,
after the victory in the First World War (1918).

The historic centre of Riva presents characteristics of a
vivacious and lively town, and is a typical town of the
region, as can be seen by the numerous buildings of Lom-
bardic-Venetian style, while the evocative *Market Square*
reproposes a recurring element in the typology of the
urban centres of Triveneto. There are numerous cultural,
musical and folkloristic attractions; above the whole
town rises the phantasmagorical ''Notte di Fiaba'' (Night
of Fables) which transforms the town with its picturesque
effects of images, lights, and colours with illuminations,
fireworks and performances in the squares. The historic
nucleus of Riva del Garda gravitates around the small
ancient port, whose boundaries are defined by the *Square
Catena* (so-called because of the implements with which
in olden times the landing of ships was prevented every

night) and *the third of November*. Onto this square faces the suggestive **Tower Apponale** built from big square blocks of stone in the 13th century and gradually raised higher and higher during the 15th - 17th centuries, with the addition of the crowning-piece which rises up from the balcony, relieved by mullioned windows. The tower, dominated by the characteristic *Anzolim* (little angel) which rotates, according to the winds, has become a symbol of Riva del Garda. The **Pretorio Palace** is an elegant 14th century construction, built in the Della Scala era by Cansignorio della Scala. Also to be seen are the big commemorative arches of the arcade which contain the plaques ascertaining the Roman, Veronese and Venetian dominations of the town. Nearby is the **Town Hall** built before the 13th century and rebuilt by the Venetians in the second half of the 15th century. In this building lived the Superintendent of the lagoon town.

The **Fortress** is a huge quadrilateral fortification, reinforced by corner towers with a keep and central arcaded court. Its architectural structure echoes the elements present in the fortress at Sirmione. Its origins date from

On the opposite page: Riva del Garda, one of the rooms of the Civic Museum; exhibits on show; adjacent, Riva del Garda, the Parish Church of the Assumption; the interior of the Parish Church and detail of the main altar (below).

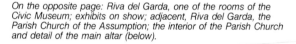

the 12th century but is was rebuilt by the Veronese in the 14th century, it was modified by the Venetians in the 15th century and underwent ulterior transformations under the dominance of the episcopal principality of Trentino and again at the time of the Austrian occupation. The imposing building which looks out onto the lake is entirely surrounded by water and is accessible by means of a drawbridge. Inside the courtyard are sarcophagi that date back to Roman times, whilst inside the building is the **Civic Museum**, which holds significant architectural testimony of the upper parts of the Garda territory, and of

To the left: Riva del Garda, the tourist port and the ferry "Verona"; the Varone falls; view of the upper section of Garda from the Riva mountains (above).

the Val di Ledro. The exhibits date back to Prehistoric times, and of particular interest are the materials discovered in a lake-dweller seat, found along the shores of the lake of Ledro, the Roman documents, the paleontological and naturalistic exhibits and evidence of an ethnographical character. The **Church of the Assumtpion** is an 18th century building, with an elegant façade in three orders, decorated by niches containing statues, and with a beautiful doorway. The interior with obvious Baroque characteristics, has a beautiful high altar and excellent paintings by 18 - 19th century artists, among whom stand out the works of G.B. Cignaroli, G. Craffonara and G.B. Piazzetta. Another interesting building is the 17th century **Church of the ''Inviolata''**, which contains paintings by Palma the Younger and frescoes by T. Turri and P. Ricchi.

Torbole: the promenade (above); the plaque and effigy dedicated to Goethe (adjacent).

TORBOLE

This town is the chief town of the commune of Nago-Torbole and looks out onto an evocative sickle-shaped bay, in the eastern part of the lakeside. The tourist who arrives here from Nago, along the road which has steep bends and which goes down towards the lake, will find a spectacle of indescribable beauty: the thin band of flat country, covered in the last hundred metres, by the river bed of the Sacra, now, near the mouth of the river, emerges verdantly on the background of the mirror of the lake, wedged between two mountain ranges and vanishes towards infinity giving the appearance of widening out into an immense sea. The flat ground is dotted with roofs of the houses, concentrated around the shore of the lake, which stand out from the green fields, making an obvious chromatic contrast with the sky-blue waters of Garda, which reflects the intense azzure tonality of the sky.

Torbole has played an important part in the naval history of the 15th century. In May 1440, the Venetians, in order

Torbole: a view of Nago; the Pot-Holes of the Giants (adjacent).

to take reinforcements to Riva, which was in the hands of the Visconti family at the time, and to relieve the pressure of the Milanese on Brescia devised an ingenious diversion tactic which took the adversaries by surprise and which cost them a bitter defeat in the waters of the lake. Going back up the course of the Adige, with a flottila, by then taken to pieces and transported until Torbone, they afterwards put the ships back together again, with the aid of several hundred oxen, in the town, and then after lauching the ships, went back to defeat the Visconti fleet. At the end of the summer of 1786, the great poet Goethe, at the beginning of his unforgettable journey in Italy, stayed at Torbole, giving in his writings, a nostalgic and passionate image of the lake which still today continues to be the main tourist attraction for the hoardes of German-speaking holidaymakers.

Amongst the major tourist attractions of Torbole are the **Plaque and Effigy dedicated to Goethe** placed on the arcaded building where the illustrious literary man lived, commemorated also by a *bust* on the lakeside. The

Windsurfing attracts many enthusiasts to Lake Garda.

Church of St. Andrea is divided by three aisles and contains valuable wooden choir stalls. But the most important artistic element is without doubt a superb 18th century painting done by G.B. Cignaroli which depicts the *Martyring of St. Andrea*. A little south of Torbole, flows in the mirror of the lake, the artificial gallery excavated between Adige and Garda and which serves to regulate the impetuous floods of the river Adige, allowing the downflow of the waters into the nearby lake of Garda. A pleasant stroll brings one to the ruins of **Penede Castle**, destroyed in the 18th century when it was once in the possession of the Serene Republic.

One site which particularly excites naturalists and geologists is to be found near the bends and turnings of the road which leads to Nago: the so-called **Marmitte dei Giganti** which represents a tangible display of the erosive phenomena of ample capacity which took place during the Ice Age when an enormous glacier covered the whole territory. The pot-holes, as they are called, are in fact shafts formed by glaciers, determined by the swirling rotation of boulders and glacial debris which percipitated from the upper strata.

MALCESINE

The town is the major centre of the Veronese Coast of Olives so-called, because of the great number of these plants that grow spontaneously and vigorously in this area. Almost on the border with the province of Trento, it is made up of a picturesque aglomeration of residences dating back to various times, and it stretches out towards the lake, on a small promontory dominated by the scenic outline of turretted and battlemented Veronese fortifications. The landscape of the upper basin of Garda is characterised by the mountains opposite where the false plains of Tremosine and Tignale become displaced. Behind the town rises, all of a sudden, the massive profile of Mt. Baldo which reaches 2218 metres at Cima Valdritta and which constitutes a district for skiing, for excursions and for naturalists of great renown. Towards the south, a gentle inlet opens up faced by the tiny island of the Olive, whilst towards the north the upper portion of the lake looms up, wedged, like a fjord amongst the mountains, and marked by the characteristic profile of Mt. Brione. An unusual explanation for the origin of the present day

place-name makes reference to the Latin name *Silex* meaning a "paved road of large worked stone". Archeological exhibits found on the site have proved the presence of the Romans in the town, as the tombs and funeral objects (coins and everyday utensils) seem to testify. In the Early Medieval times the town was not subjected too much to the succession of Barbaric invasions. Already the seat of fortified complexes during the time of the Longobards and the French, Malcesine began to be a part of the territories administrated by the Veronese Episcopacy, thereafter passing under the control of the Scaligeri. At the time of the domination of the Lords of Verona, the fortress was restructured and afterwards the institution "Captains of the Lake" was created, which, would have jurisdictional power over the centres of the Veronese parts of Garda, between the 16th and the 18th centuries. Around the middle of September 1786, the famous Wolfang von Goethe found himself passing through the place during the course of his famous journey. Attracted by the beauty of the location, while trying to draw the outline of the castle to use later as material and documentation for his writings, he was surrounded by some suspicious peasants who, believing him to be a spy, nearly had him imprisoned.

Malcesine: a panoramic view towards the upper basin of the lake and Mt. Brione.

Nowadays the outline of the fortress is one of the motifs most frequently photographed by tourists, mainly German-speaking, showing the enormous fascination that Malcesine and its lake has exerted on the Nordic population since the time of Goethe. The town is counted as being one of the most luminous pearls in the spectacular "necklace" of tourist centres which are scattered along the perimeter of Garda. It can cater for tourists extremely well, and has excellent hotels, capable of accomodating numerous visitors and also offers several typical restaurants where the exquisite specialities of the Garda cuisine can be tasted, accompanied by the excellent wines of the Veronese coast. Due to its extremely pleasant geographical position, it boasts an exceptionally mild and moderate climate, and retains its favourable properties even in the colder months, and is for this reason, a well-known holiday and health resort throughout each season of the year. The sunny slopes are populted by olive groves that descend right down to the shores of the lake, whilst here and there, rise the characteristic outlines of cypress trees

On the opposite page: Malcesine, the port (above); the Palace of the Captains of the Lake (below); the Scaligero Castle which dominates the town (above).

which seem to have been placed to guard the castle. The tourist who arrives from the North is immediately impressed by the sharp contrast of climate and vegetation which here take on a luxuriant Mediterranean aspect. The outskirts of Malcesine are of great naturalistic interest: marked footpaths that wind along the mountain sides, in a fabulous scenario of indescribably scenic suggestion, and a steep cable-car system in two sections, allows one to reach the extremely scenic and spectacular peak of Mt. Baldo.

The **Palace of the Captains of the Lake** shows a decidedly Venetian influence and has an elegant façade with beautiful windows and is crowned with merlons. The first construction dates back to the Veronese period, when it rose up on a pre-existent structure of Roman times. Subsequently gone to ruin it was reconstructed in the second half of the 15th century, giving hospitality (starting from the following century) to the various Captains of the Lake, who followed one another in succession up until the fall of the Venetian Republic. Inside the building the *Meeting Room* stands out, and it is here that the insigna of the Captains are kept, and decorations of the 16th century also catch the visitors eye.

The **Scaligero Castle** has the appearance of a battlemented fortress which is set on the outermost projection of the promontary. It is surmounted by a slender tower and,

Malcesine: a view of the Scaligero Castle (above); the Scaligero Castle, the keep (adjacent).

seen from the lake, appears, at times, both picturesque and ghostly, on the peak of a precipitous wall projecting out into the lake. The massive fortification dominates the ancient and evocative nucleus of Malcesine; from the top of its tower one can admire an unrestricted view which ranges from the uppermost part of Garda, set among the mountains, right down to the Brescian coast, which includes the lovely centre of Limone and the opposite town of Pieve, seat of the commune of Tremosine. This enchanting panoramic sight stretches southwards where the enormous "mirror" of water begins almost imperceptibly to widen out, whilst behind the town the grandiose bulk of Mt. Baldo seems to constitute ulterior natural defence for the town of the Veronese Riviera. On the site of the present-day castle, there once existed an ancient fortress, some traces of which can still be seen today in the walls. Towards the end of the 6th century it was completely destroyed and was then rebuilt in Carlovingian times and was transformed into a castle during the years of the Veronese domination. Subsequent bulwark of the Visconti family, it then became an outpost of the Serene Republic of San Marco, which held it, up until the end of the 18th century. Starting from 1815 it was transformed by the Austrians, who used it as a fortress for defending the nearby border. Inside the castle is the **History Museum of Malcesine** which holds important evidence of archeological interest discovered in the district and refers back to the Pre-Roman and Medieval periods.

Malcesine: The History Museum of Malcesine, one of the rooms of the interior, exhibits on show (adjacent).

Worthy of mention are the collections of arms, the prints, the publications, the naturalist collections and the Risorgimento relics. In one room, the remains of a boat, found at the bottom of the lake, have been put on view. In the same room the ingenious diversive manoeuvre which permitted the Venetians to surprise the flottila of the Visconti family, in the famous lake battle of Torbole, has been reconstructed. In a courtyard stands *the bust of Johann Wolfgang von Goethe*, erected to commemorate his presence in Malcesine in September 1786 and to recall the unusual episode already mentioned, in which he took part, much against his will.

The **Church of Saint Stephen** is a building in decidedly 18th century style but its origins are even more remote and go back, in fact, to the Carlovingian era. All traces are lost of the ancient site of worship, but we know that it contained the moral remains of the hermit saints Benigno and Caro. In the first half of the 14th century the church underwent restoration work and in the second half of the same century, work was begun on the porch of the rectory which we can still see today. In the first half of the 18th century the demolition of the ancient building took place, on the site of which, rose up the present church. The interior is enriched by numerous elements of considerable artistic merit, but the most important is still *The Deposition of Christ* painted by Girolamo dai Libri, and which was transferred here from the Veronese church of *Santa Maria in Organo*.

In the piazza that gives onto the picturesque little port is situated the **Church of St. Nicolò and St. Rocco**, the building was planned by G. Zorzi and was built in the first half of the 17th century. In the upper part of the suburb stands the 16th century **Church of St. Benigno and St. Caro**. Another place of worship of exceptional interest is the **Church of the Madonna**, otherwise known as the *Church of the Fountain*. The building owes its present appearance to restructuring and extension work carried out in the 17th century, to enable the church to accomodate the ever increasing numbers of pilgrims and devoted worshippers. The name of Church of the Fountain derives from a spring of water, believed to be miraculous, which is to be found under a rectangular stone, in the middle of the floor.

All the communal territory of Malcesine presents aspects of substantial touristic and artistic interest; to the south of the chieftown, in the hamlet of Cassone stands the **Church of San Zenone in Monte**, which is situated in an evocative position, in an unapproachable and deserted spot. In the same place stand the two churches dedicated to **St. Benigno and St. Caro**, one of which dates back to the end of the 15th century. The 18th century **Church** stands out because of its original octagonal nave, whilst the belltower dates back to the last years of the last century. Off Cassone is the **Island of Trimelone** on whose ground stands, since the Barbaric era (10th century), a fortress erected by the Ungari. In the second half of the 12th century, Federico Barbarossa set fire to the castle during the course of a military manoeuvre. In the era of the della Scala family of Verona, the castle was restored by the Lords of Verona who left here their own coat of arms. In contemporary times, the ancient ruins were destroyed so as to enable the building of a modern fortified structure, which, during the course of the Second World War, was lost. In the hamlet of Navene, to the north of the chief town, stands the 17th century **Church of St. Maria di Navene**, already mentioned in acts dating back to the 11th century. In the town of Val Casera is situated the **Church of St. Michael**, of ancient Medieval origins, already mentioned in the 12th century, and reconstructed at the end of the 16th century and also at the beginning of the 20th century. Amongst the numerous 20th century villas, built primarily during the first years of the century, note should be made of the *Villa Gruber*, the *Villa Labia*, the *Villa Molitor*, the *Villa Noli*, the *Villa Bianca*, the *Villa Nichesola*, the *Villarose*, the *Villa Sogno*, the *Villa delle Rondini*, the *Villa Irma and Giulia* and the *Villa Lombardi*.

Particularly interesting is the excursion to **Mt. Baldo**, which can be made by cable-car, which goes over beautiful scenery, and leads to the *Baita dei Forti*, 1745 metres, near the Bocca Tratto Spin, on the ridge of the mountain. The panorama, which one can see from here, is extremely impressive, particularly at sunrise and at sunset, when the vivid, burning tonality of the sunlight covers the peaks of the distant snow-covered mountains, while at the bottom, the boundless mirrors of the lake, stretch out, nestling between the mountains, upon which Malcesine faces out, and which seen from above, seems to be lost between the green woods and the cerulean azzure of the waters of Garda.

Adjacent: Malcesine, the Parish Church of St. Stephan; "Deposition" of Girolamo dai Libri (below); on the opposite page, Malcesine as seen from the cable cars which run along Mt. Baldo; the upper river basin of Garda from the mountain cablecar station (below).

MOUNT BALDO

This splendid panoramic balcony constitutes one of the most remarkable mountainous formations and stretches out along the whole of the Garda Territory. Its imposing bulk dominates the eastern part of Garda, from Torri del Benaco until Torbole, giving an extremely characteristic stamp to the Garda landscape, often marked by its picturesque snow-covered outline. On its slopes, are numerous ski-resorts, while a great number of paths allow us to explore the mountain, the region also being known as the *Botanical Gardens of Italy*, due to the enormous variety and abundance of rare vegetable species.

CASTELLETTO DI BRENZONE

The town is one of several which make up the outstretched commune of Brensone, picturesquely laid out amongst the slopes of Mt. Baldo, and has, in recent years, enjoyed an ever-increasing tourist trade. The stamp of the landscape is dominated by the olive groves, which emerge with the Mediterranean vegetation. The most important tourist spot is the **Church of San Zeno**, an interesting Romanesque construction, made up of two apses, built in the 12th century. It also has a linear belltower decorated with mullioned windows and dominated by a square cusp. In the lunette of the protiro (entrance hall) in the façade can be seen the frescoe of *Christ benedicting* (14th century).

The ski runs on Mount Baldo (above); Castelletto di Brenzone, Church of San Zeno (left); on the right, view of Malcesine at night (above); boats moored at Torri del Benaco.

TORRI DEL BENACO

A luminous pearl of the Riviera of the Olives, it is situated along the Eastern part of Garda, where the outline of Garda visibly widens out. Behind the town, stretch out the hills which prelude the long range of Mt. Baldo. In front of Torri, the promontary of Maderno-Toscolano stretches out into the lake; the town is linked to Maderno by regular car-ferries, thereby avoiding the car journey around the coast. From the panoramic lakeside, one can see the opposite towns on the western part of Garda, and Gardone Riviera, and onto the enchanting gulf of Salò, bordered in the south by the upper promontary of the Valténesi, which stretches out towards the lake, which is faced by the beautiful island of Garda.

The first human settlment in the area of Torri dates back to the lake-dwelling period, but even in Roman times we have evidence of a town named *Castrum Turrium*, reference point for the travellers who passed along the Via Claudia Augusta, heading towards the north. Recorded in the so-called "Table of Cles" as the chief town of the Tulliassi peoples, in the Early Middle Ages it played host to Berengario the First, depending for a long time on Garda, which at the time was in hands of the Germanic

Torri del Benaco: a panoramic view and the port (above); the Scaligero Castle (adjacent).

invaders. Afterwards it became the possession of the Della Scala family, and then became a part of the ever-increasing number of territories governed by the Venetians. It subsequently became the settlement of the Captains of the Lake sharing from the 9th century, with Malcesine, important administrative prerogatives over the whole territory of the eastern part of Garda.

The Torri of today is an esteemed tourist and residential town, blessed with excellent services and other facilities which cater for sport and leisure activities. During the summer months its harbour is overflowing with offshore navigation, whilst the surrounding areas of the town offer pleasant and interesting excursions in a district which has been the site on which important pre-historic findings have been discovered and which is characterised by interesting rocky incisions. The turretted **Castle**, characterised by Ghibelline battlements, stands in a beautiful setting facing the lake. There already existed, on the site, fortifications of Roman origin which were also spread out around the neighbouring area of the port. At the end of the 9th century Berengario supervised the restructuring of the defensive aspect of Torri, with the enlargement of the town walls. During Medieval times the Castle acted as host to the Order of Magistrates known as the "Gardesana dell'Acqua" and was subsequently reinforced by the Della Scala family who built two additional towers to the Roman ones, which can still be seen today, in a position which dominates the wet-dock. Due to its urban character the ancient nucleus of the town is very important, and

Torri del Benaco: the Eccheli Palace (above); the tower of Berengario (adjacent).

has several historical buildings such as the *Eccheli Palace* (15th century) and the so-called *Berengario Tower*, a square Medieval construction which is set on the site of the ruins of an ancient church. The **Parish church** was already mentioned in documents of the 12th century and the second half of the 15th century and was dedicated to St. Peter and St. Paul. The present day church was finished during the first half of the 18th century, planned by the architect Antonio Spiazzi who had already worked on the one at Salò. The front of the building, in two orders, is vertically decorated with pilaster strips and has niches containing statues; it is crowned by a triangular typanium. The bell-tower contemporary to the final construction of the building, is set on the foundations of the tower of the ancient defence system devised by Berengario. In the *Calderini Square* is an ancient 15th century building, once the seat of the Captaincy, and today it has become a hotel. Onto the same piazza faces the **Church of the Fallen**, known once as the *Church of the Trinity*; its construction dates back to the 14th century. In its interior, once, the religious rites were performed, in conjunction with the meetings of the Council of Gardesana, and it is adorned with frescoes which are in a good state of preservation. In the district there are numerous buildings of both artistic and architectural interest. A little way outside the town, near the cemetery stands the **Church of St. John**; its most remote origins going back to the Romanesque period, whilst the most recent transformation took place in the 18th century. In the interior some valuable 14th century frescoes can be seen, believed to be the

Torri del Benaco: the façade of the Parish Church (adjacent); a small square in the centre of the town and the Church dedicated to the Fallen (below).

*Torri del Benaco: a panoramic view towards the lake (above);
sunset over the port (adjacent).*

work of Giovanni da Bardolino, together with a 15th
century fresco, in all probability, painted by Morone.
The **Church of Saint Anthony** dates back to the 14th century, when it was known as *S. Maria delle Tezze*. Transformed and extended in the second half of the 17th century, it was then consecrated to the present patron saint. A
valuable fresco on the outside of the church representing
a *View of Torri del Benaco in the 17th century* can be seen,
while other frescoes date back to a period between the
15th and 17th centuries. The **Church of Saint Faustino
and Saint Giovita** was already sited in acts dating back to
the 15th century, but probably its origins are even more
remote. The interior has 15th century style frescoes which
depict *The Madonna with Child* and *Saint Rocco and
Saint Sebastian*, and the sepulchre of the hermit Pietro
Malerba who lived during the 15th century. Finally the
hamlets of Pai and Albisano are worthy of mention. In
the former interesting churches such as that of *Saint Mark*
and the old *Church of Saint Gregory* can be seen. The
New Church dates back to the 16th century and rises on
the site of a chapel which formed part of the ancient
castle. Albisano is a charming little hillside town which
enjoys the advantages of its enviable geographic location.
This is one of the panoramic observation posts which is
most frequented by tourists in the whole area of the
Veronese portion of Garda. Here we can see the **Church
of Saint Martin**, already mentioned in the 13th century
and thereafter frequently restructured. The **Parish
Church** dates back to the 18th century.

GARDA

Amongst the numerous jewels that are set along the Veronese coast of Garda, Garda excells for its vibrating notes of colour and landscape, both elements which, make it one of the most sought after and visited tourist spots of the entire Garda territory. The small town looks out over an enchanting bay, guarded by the rocky outline of the Rocca and characterized by the splendid Punta San Vigilio. The latter from a morphological point of view, could be defined as an appendix to the orographical system of the Baldo mountain range, stretching out even to the waters of the lake: to the north it looks out to the magnificent bay of Sirene, a romantic cove, where the green olive trees slope down to the edge of the lake, interspersed with the dark outline of cypress trees, pines and by thick luxuriant vegetation. Over everything dominates the blueness, sometimes intense, sometimes turquoise of a Garda, that here acquires the dimensions and ferocity of a "sea" often hit by the winds and shaken by almost deep-sea waves. For its mild lakeside climate, exhaulted

Garda: panorama of the town looking out onto the gulf (above); the promenade towards the Fortress (adjacent); on the opposite page, a panoramic glimpse of the Fortress.

by reliefs which act as a natural barrier against the cold southern currents, Garda is a health resort like few others, favoured above all, by a large Germanic clientele. The wealth of its artistic patrimony its historical connections, the great magnificence of its villas and residences, all contribute in making Garda an excellent tourist centre, which is well known, thanks to the validity of the comprehensive structures and services. The origins of Garda go back as far as the Prehistoric age, when a large amount of lake dwellings were constructed here. Subsequently it became a Roman centre, and was well known throughout the Longobard and French eras. In those days, the German word *Warte* used to mean "look-out post" with obvious reference to the ancient fortress inside which

Left: Punta San Vigilio (above); view of Garda extending over the lake (below); view of the port (above).

Adelaide di Borgogna was imprisoned in the 10th century. The actual place name seems to derive from this term which in those times started out being used to define the Italian lake, substituting the Latin root word *Benacus*. Passing under the control of the Veronese and then under the Venetians, the town was the seat of Giudicaria Gardense for a long time; an administrative entity which also governed many parts of the hinterland. Amongst the numerous architectural manifestations of prevalent Venetian style the **Palace of the Captains of the Lake** should be mentioned; a beautiful building whose front is decorated with beautiful windows with trilobe arches and which stands out because of the low porches on the ground floor. The building, which once looked out onto the brimming waters of the lake, now looks out onto a delightful small piazza which is enriched by greenery and in which the groups of tourists arrange to meet and sit down at the cafe tables. Starting from the 15th century the Palazzo was the seat of the Corporazione degli Originari. Another small building which bears traces of the

Garda: the Palace of the Captains of the Lake (above); the Fregoso Palace (adjacent).

Venetian influence is the **Fregoso Palace**, a 15th century building which today boasts a beautiful front enriched by mullioned windows which are dominated by a large arch under which runs the road. On the left of the building an external staircase leads to the entrance doorway which has a tympanum.

The **former Carlotti Palace** is a building stamped with remarkable Renaissance forms which once had a garden overlooking the lake. What remains of the building shows the typical traits given to it in all probability by the Renaissance architect Michele Sanmicheli. Also *the Loggia*, which was once a dock, a lookout post of this residential complex, allows the stamp of the great Veronese architect to shine through. A little way outside the town amidst the green of a scenic park the **Villa Canossa** looks out over the lake. A jewel of Renaissance architecture, it was built in the 16th century and belongs to the House of Carlotti. It owes its present aspect to 19th century work

Adjacent: the loggia/lodge of the Former Carlotti Palace; the "Palio" (Festival) of the Town Districts (below left); a view of the centre (below right).

which was carried out by the architect Franco. The building is marked by traits of great magnificence and pomp which are however all balanced, allowing the building to blend in magnificently with the natural surroundings of wild beauty. Another superlative residence of this splendid coast area is the **Villa Albertini**, set in pleasant surroundings in the centre of this evocative gulf. The building of 15th - 16th century origins was once the House of Bercelli and was substantially transformed in the 18th century. Its stamp is made typical by a mixture of styles and architectural harmonies which make the Late Medieval building stand out, in the battlemented corner towers, and classical traits, of vague Paladian style, in the front crowned by a triangular tympanum. The magnificent park is full of ornamental motifs. On the magnificent Punta San Vigilio stands the 16th **Villa Guarienti**, built by Agostino Brenzone. The open gallery of the Italian Garden is attributed to Sanmicheli.

On the opposite page: Garda, the Carlotti Palace (above); Villa Canossa (below); Villa Albertini (adjacent); Punta S. Vigilio, Villa Guarienti (below).

BARDOLINO

The town is a pleasant health resort in the Veronese part of Garda which looks out on an enchanting sickle shaped bay between Lazise and Garda. Bardolino is famous for its wine bearing the same name (DOC wine) which is produced in limited territory and carefully chosen vineyards. The care taken with the grape harvesting is also an essential element in the treatment of the grape which is largely practised and diffused.

All around the luxuriant olive groves stretch out as far as the eye can see. These groves produce a refined oil of great value. The climate, exceptionally mild all through the year, and particularly through the winter months makes the town a centre of attraction for tourists and holiday makers, mostly German speaking. Although a legend unites the origins of Bardolino with the myth of Troy, we know for certain, that in all probability it was firstly a lake-dweller seat, then it became populated by Alpine folk and then came under the control of Rome. It was a free commune during Medieval times (12th century) and was for a long time under the control of the Della Scala family of Verona.

The hamlet of Cisano looks out onto the lake in the south of the chief town. Its main characteristic is the Romanesque **Church of S. Maria**, a higly valuable construction of the 12th century, but originally built in the 8th century. One notes the front, enriched by a mullioned window and by a small protiro (entrance hall) which is

Bardolino: the port (above); Cisano, The Parish Church of St. Mary (adjacent).

sustained by columns which dominate the portal. Architecturally interesting are the adjacent bell-tower and the exterior of the apse. The repeated restructuring of the interior has unfortunately irreparably altered the physiognomy.

At Bardolino we can see the **Church of S. Severo** which is counted as being one of the best expressions of Romanesque architecture in the Veronese territory. The building, originally of the 13th century, thanks to precise and careful restoration work has been restored to its ancienti splendour, and the worrying irreversible degradation, which started in the last century has been stopped. At first destined to be used as a theatre, and then revalued for its ancient architectural dignity (between the 1920 - 1930) it is today a magnificent Romanesque complex, which stands out because of the harmonious structures of the valuable tripartite apse, for the simple front, enriched by a small protiro dominating the entrance, and for the outstanding cuspidated belltower. The interior is characterized by the tripartition of the nave and is decorated by a remarkable cycle of frescoes in the Romanesque style.

Amongst the other churches in the area, the **Chapel of San Zeno** situated at the beginning of the eastern part of Garda, stands out. Built between the 8th and the 9th centuries, it is considered to be an excellent piece of evidence of Carlovingian architecture. It is a building with an unusual cross-shaped plan, which shows, in the workings of the capitals, evident links with the skilled workers of Lombardy, who were active in the Venetian territory, and who, in all probability were influenced by the experience of the Masters of Como (architects and sculptors).

Bardolino: the Church of St. Severo, a view of the tripartite apse and the belltower (adjacent); the Chapel of St. Zeno and its interior (below).

LAZISE

This is an evocative example of a town which is still largely contained within its medieval town walls. Lazise looks
out on the eastern shore of Garda, at the point where the
lake is at its largest, restricted by the gentle and fertile
hills which constitute a morainic amphitheatre of Garda.
An ancient lake-dwelling seat, it was a Roman *pagus*
named *Lasitium* (from lacus-meaning lake), becoming a
free commune with many autonomistic prerogatives.
Starting from the end of the 12th century it was acquired
by the della Scala family from whom it was captured by
the Visconti family. Coming under Venetian domination
it was subjected to various vicissitudes up until national
unification.

The turreted **Scaligero Castle** with its walls which are
crowned with merlons, forms part of a circuit of medieval
fortifications - the 14th century *New Gate*. The **Customs
House**, otherwise known as *darsena* (dock) is a valuable
example of Venetian engineering, connected to the ancient port system. The Romanesque **Church of S. Nicolò**
is flanked by the picturesque and evocative harbour,
where the characteristic fishing boats are moored. It was
built in the 12th century and contains an interesting cycle
of 14th century frescoes. The belltower is the result of an
18th century reconstruction.

On the opposite page: Lazise, the Customs-House or dock
(above); the Scaligero Castle (below); an evening view of the
port (above); the Church of St. Nicolò (adjacent).

PESCHIERA

Due to its particular geographic position, at the crossroads of important roads, it has always been an attractive datum point, both in the strategic and in the military sense. The town is frequently visited by holiday-makers and is very intersting from a tourist point of view. As it is easily reached by train and by car, it has become one of the main entrance gates into the Garda region. Its fertile hinterland includes a famous zone where the Lugana bianco (white wine) is produced.

Being an ancient prehistoric seat, it constituted one of the many pile-dweller villages which joined together many centres in the Garda area, at least during the primitive age. Colonized by the Romans, who called it *Arilica*, it was reinforced by fortifications, whilst still being an important centre for fishing and transport. Named *Pischaria* in Medieval times, with evident reference to the abundance of marine fauna, it was an autonomous commune depending firstly on the Veronese Episcopacy and the on the Della Scala family (of Verona). Reinforced by the Venetians, who made it into a fortified stronghold, it then became part of the Cisalpina Republic, and was subjected to various vicissitutes before coming under the control of the Austrians. In the Risorgimento era, it formed part of the invincible "Quadrilatero" together with Verona, Mantua and Legnago. The stamp of Austro-Hungarian fortifications still today characterize the town as one of the best examples of a military stronghold of the 19th century. Only a few traces are left of the *Fortress*, with its connotations of Dante, whilst the powerful bulwark of the **Mura** (town walls), which have a pentagonal shape and which reach down as far as the edge of the lake, is still intact. The town walls, covered by thick vegetation and shaded by trees make up a remarkable observation post, looking out on the lower Garda basin. Other places of interest include the **Verona Gate**, planned by Sanmicheli, and the ancient **Brescia Gate**: both have a remarkably imposing appearance.

The **Sanctuary of the Madonna of Frassino**, stands a short distance away from the town. This is a 16th century construction, which today has been declared a national monument, and stands on the site of where, it is believed, a miracle occured. Afterwards the Francescans built a conventual complex in the neighbourhood. The simple front has a rose-window and is preceded by an arcade with frescoes dating from the 17th century. Inside we can see the miraculous statue of the *Madonna*, 17th century frescoes by Farinati and the paintings by Zenon Veronese, by B. Muttoni and by A. Bertanza.

Peschiera: view towards the port (above); on the right, ancient walls along the lake; the Sanctuary of Madonna del Frassino (above); view of the port with two tourist boats.

GARDALAND

A few years ago on the road that leads from Peschiera to Pacengo, Gardaland, a town of recreation and entertainment was built. This important infrastructure is a great tourist attraction and draws people from many parts of the territory. The various attractions are evocatively set in natural verdant scenery, which has the natural background of the lake. A small train and a cable-car allows one to look out over this little "Disneyland" of the Verona area, which has also recently been extended to the delight of both adults and children alike.

ZOO AND SAFARI PARK OF GARDA

Amongst the many places of interest for tourists in the Veronese district of Garda, the Zoo and Safari Park of Garda, near Pastrengo should be mentioned. The realization of this initiative was carried out by the architect Alberto Avesani, who, on his own grounds has collected together rare and precious specimens of fauna. The animals are allowed to roam freely around an area of remarkable beauty, and visitors are asked to stay in their cars so as not to disturb the animals.

*Above: the Amusement Park "Gardaland" near Pacengo;
Pastrengo, the Zoo/Safari Park of Garda (adjacent).*

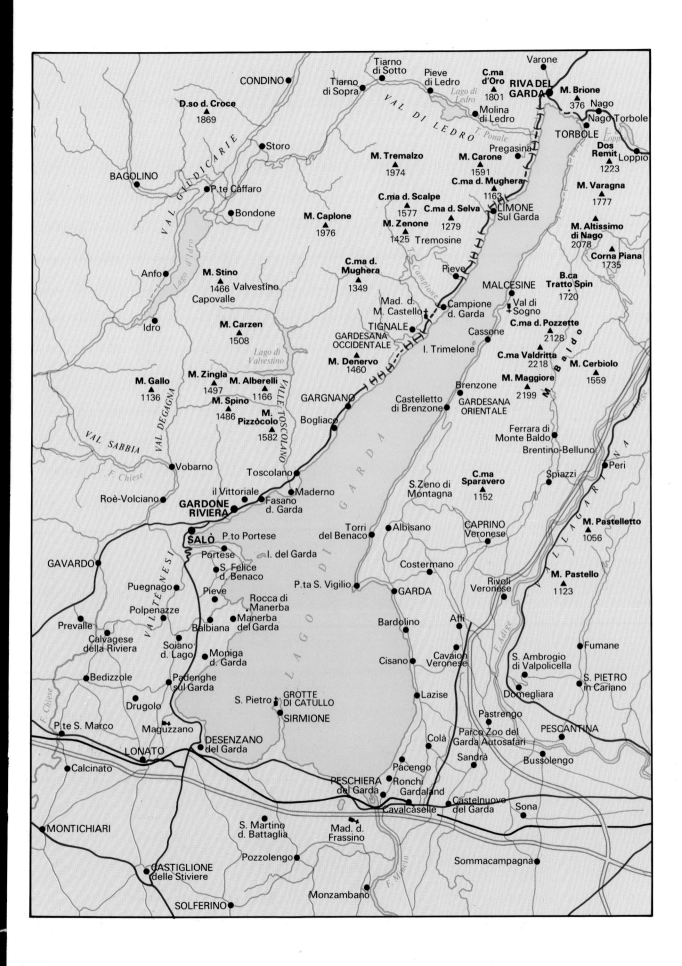

CONTENTS